M. S. Burton
50 Cramworth St,
W. 2.

THE ENGLISH ASSOCIATION

President, 1941: THE RT. HON. VISCOUNT SAMUEL, G.C.B., D.C.L.
Chairman of Committee: NOWELL SMITH, M.A.

AIMS AND ACTIVITIES

1. To unite and introduce to one another those who are interested in English Language and Literature whether as writers, teachers, artists, actors, or administrators, and to act as a link between groups engaged in specialised English work.

2. To uphold the standards of English writing and speech, to contribute to English letters, scholarship, and research, to discuss methods of English teaching, and to encourage specially the work of younger members.

3. To put these aims into practice by providing lectures, readings, discussions, social functions, and a magazine, and to organise occasional visits to dramatic performances and places of literary interest.

(*a*) The financial year runs from January 1 to December 31, and a subscription paid at any time during the year entitles a member to the Association's magazine ENGLISH (three numbers) and the Presidential Address.

(*b*) The annual subscription to the Central Body is 10s. 6d., or with *Essays and Studies* and *The Year's Work in English Studies* (post free), £1 1s. Life Membership (which does not cover *Essays and Studies* and *The Year's Work in English Studies*) is £5. Life Membership subscription can be compounded on the basis of a deduction of 1s. 6d. for every annual subscription paid.

(*c*) The annual subscription of a full member of a Branch is fixed within certain limits by the Branch, and is usually 7s. 6d., or 17s. 6d.

(*d*) Members of the Association are entitled to purchase the Annual Bibliography of the Modern Humanities Research Association at the reduced members' price of 4s. 6d., post free, non-members' price being 8s. 6d. Application should be made to the Acting Secretary of the English Association, 3, Cromwell Road, London, S.W.7.

(*e*) Subscriptions to the Central Body should be made out in favour of the English Association and sent to Barclay's Bank Ltd., 95, Victoria Street, Westminster, S.W.1. Further information will be given to intending members, or they will be placed in communication with the Hon. Secretary of any Branch, by the Acting Secretary, 3, Cromwell Road, London, S.W.7.

Poems of To-Day :

Second Series

Poems of To-Day:

Second Series

London :
Published for the English Association
by Sidgwick & Jackson, Ltd., 1941

First issued in May, 1922
Reprinted, July and September, 1922
January and September, 1923
January and November, 1924
August and October, 1925
June and July, 1928
July and August, 1929
May, 1931
May, 1933
May and October, 1934
May, 1936
July, 1941

Made and Printed in Great Britain by
Hazell, Watson & Viney, Ltd., London and Aylesbury.

PREFATORY NOTE

THE welcome accorded to the first volume of "Poems of To-day" leads the Committee to hope that a second volume may be of service to those interested in the poetry of their own times. The first volume was published in August, 1915; the interval that has passed has brought to all experience which the imagination of a few has transmuted into poetry. This second volume is an attempt to bring together such poems as represent, not indeed all the shifting tendencies of the period, but those moods which have proved most permanent, persisting through all the changes of events and of public feeling, linking the poetry of to-day with that of yesterday, and looking forward to the poetry of to-morrow.

Most of the selections are from the writings of younger men, who have written mainly under the influences and reactions of the war; but others are from the works of older and more established poets who have not lost touch with this generation. Living poets whose outlook and method belong to the earlier rather than to the second decade of the century do not come within the scope of the anthology, but poems by writers now dead have been admitted, where for reasons of copyright such writers were excluded from the first volume or inadequately represented there.

For the choice and arrangement of the poems, the war necessarily provides the starting-point. The moods of war are shown, occasionally as they have been realised in the first crude shock of actual encounter, but more often as they have been deepened and stabilised in the impassioned memories of the poet. From the war, men's minds have turned to England, sometimes with pride in her past, sometimes with doubt for her future, but never with despair. The poets have paid tribute to the hold upon them of school and college and home, of green countryside and rolling downland, of heroic memories and well-loved associations. The poetry of nature shows a strength of local feeling that escapes from the limits of provincial sentiment by its unassuming but deep-rooted sincerity. With the love of nature is found a sympathy with animals half-humorous, half tender. The sense of fellowship and the love of life are the more marked because of the events which have threatened both, but love between man and woman is a less distinctive note in the poetry of the day. Romance is blended with realism, and escape is made from modern conventions and modern conditions, sometimes by looking back into the past, more often by way of the sea and far wanderings, sometimes by magic. Finally, the mystery of death has quickened men's perception of the mystery of life and of the immanence of spirit.

January, 1922.

INDEX OF AUTHORS

For permission to use copyright poems, the English Association is greatly indebted to the authors; to the literary executors of F. W. Bourdillon (Mrs. Bourdillon), Rupert Brooke (Mr. E. H. Marsh), T. E. Brown (Mrs. Brown), A. H. Bullen (Miss E. Lister), "Michael Field" (Mr. T. Sturge Moore), J. E. Flecker (Mrs. Flecker), Julian Grenfell (Lady Desborough), W. N. Hodgson (Miss Hodgson), Francis Ledwidge (Lord Dunsany), F. W. Moorman (Mrs. Moorman), J. M. Plunkett (Mrs. Plunkett), C. H. Sorley (Professor W. R. Sorley), Sir Cecil Spring-Rice (Mr. Bernard Holland), E. Wyndham Tennant (Lady Glenconner), Edward Thomas (Mrs. Thomas), Francis Thompson (Mr. Wilfrid Meynell), and T. P. Cameron Wilson (Rev. T. Wilson); and to the following publishers in respect of the poems enumerated:

Messrs. Allen & Unwin :
    Beatrice Mayor, *Poems* (No. 39).
    Gilbert Murray, *The Hippolytus of Euripides* (No. 115).

Messrs. G. Bell & Sons, Ltd. :
    Michael Field, *Callirrhoë and Fair Rosamund* (No. 76).

Mr. Basil Blackwell :
    Aldous Huxley, *The Defeat of Youth* (No. 53).
    M. Nightingale, *Verses Wise and Otherwise* (No. 124).
    E. W. Tennant, *Worple Flit* (No. 10).

Messrs. W. Blackwood & Sons :
    Moira O'Neill, *Songs of the Glens of Antrim* (No. 64).

Messrs. Burns, Oates & Washbourne, Ltd.
    G. K. Chesterton, *Poems* (No. 98).
    Alice Meynell, *Poems* (Nos. 93, 138).
    F. Thompson, *Poetry of* (Nos. 30, 78, 139, 140).

Messrs. Chatto & Windus :
    Aldous Huxley, *Leda* (No. 31).
    Robert Nichols, *Ardours and Endurances* (Nos. 1, 5, 7, 9).

Messrs. W. Collins Sons & Co., Ltd.:
 E. Shanks, *The Island of Youth* (No. 38).

Messrs. Constable & Co., Ltd.:
 F. S. Boas, *Songs of Ulster and Balliol* (No. 58).
 W. de la Mare, *Collected Poems* (Nos. 27, 41, 122, 128).
 M. C. Furse, *The Gift* (No. 29).
 R. Macaulay, *Three Days* (No. 49).
 Lady Margaret Sackville, *Selected Poems* (No. 108).

Messrs. J. M. Dent & Sons, Ltd.:
 G. K. Chesterton, *The Wild Knight* (No. 71).
 Evelyn Underhill, *Immanence* (Nos. 129, 130).
 J. E. Flecker, *Forty-two Poems* (No. 119).

Messrs. Duckworth & Co.:
 H. Belloc, *Verses* (No. 102).

Mr. W. Heinemann:
 Robert Bridges, *October and other Poems* (No. 99).
 G. Dearmer, *Poems* (No. 75).
 J. Galsworthy, *Moods, Songs, and Doggerels* (No. 51).
 S. Sassoon, *War Poems* (No. 35).

Messrs. Herbert Jenkins, Ltd.:
 F. Ledwidge, *Songs of Peace* (No. 47), and
   Songs of the Fields (No. 120).

Messrs. John Lane, Ltd.:
 E. A. Mackintosh, *The Highland Regiment* (No. 2).

Messrs. Longmans, Green & Co.:
 Eva Gore-Booth, *The One and the Many* (No. 62).
 Sir C. Spring-Rice, *Collected Poems.* ed. B. Holland (Nos. 24, 101).

Messrs. Macmillan & Co., Ltd.:
 A. E. (George Russell), *Collected Poems* (Nos. 23, 63, 132, 133).
 T. E. Brown, *Collected Poems* (Nos. 42, 97, 109).
 W. W. Gibson, *Whin* (No. 20).
 Thomas Hardy, *Collected Poems* (Nos. 22, 67, 81, 121).
 R. Hodgson, *Poems* (Nos. 40, 69, 134).
 S. R. Lysaght, *Horizons and Landmarks* (No. 44), and
   Poems of the Unknown Way (No. 91).
 James Stephens, *Adventures of Seumas Beg* (Nos. 65), and
   Songs from the Clay (Nos. 70, 85).

Mr. Elkin Mathews:
 L. Binyon, *The Four Years* (Nos. 12, 17).
 G. Bottomley, *Chambers of Imagery*, 2nd Series (Nos. 33, 55).
 W. W. Gibson, *Fires* (No. 104).
 F. W. Moorman, *Songs of the Ridings* (No. 89).

Messrs. Maunsel & Roberts, Ltd.:
 P. Colum, *Wild Earth* (Nos. 83, 90).
 S. O'Sullivan, *Poems* (No. 106).
 James Stephens, *Insurrections* (Nos. 86, 107).

Messrs. Methuen & Co., Ltd. :
  Herbert Trench, *Deirdre Wed, and other Poems* (No. 79).

Mr. John Murray :
  R. Bridges, *Poetical Works* (Nos. 50, 110).
  W. N. Hodgson, *Verse and Prose in Peace and War* (Nos. 3, 11, 26).
  Violet Jacob, *Songs of Angus* (Nos. 87, 88).
  W. M. Letts, *Songs from Leinster* (No. 74).
  Sir H. Newbolt, *Poems* (Nos. 13, 16, 113, 137).

Messrs. Grant Richards, Ltd. :
  T. Sturge Moore, *The Little School* (Nos. 28, 77).

Messrs. Martin Secker, Ltd. :
  Maurice Baring, *Poems 1914–1919* (No. 19).
  J. E. Flecker, *Collected Poems* (Nos. 21, 54, 111).

Messrs. Selwyn & Blount, Ltd. :
  J. Freeman, *Poems New and Old* (Nos. 25, 61).
  E. Thomas, *Poems* (Nos. 46, 48, 84).

Messrs. Sidgwick & Jackson, Ltd. :
  H. Asquith, *The Volunteer* (Nos. 6, 15).
  E. Blunden, *The Waggoner* (Nos. 36, 45).
  R. Brooke, *Collected Poems* (No. 96).
  A. H. Bullen, *Weeping-Cross* (Nos. 56, 105).
  J. Drinkwater, *Tides* (No. 37),
               Poems, 1908–1914 (No. 59),
               Olton Pools (No. 60), and
               Loyalties (No. 68).
  F. W. Harvey, *Gloucestershire Friends* (No. 131), and
               Ducks (No. 34).
  W. J. Turner, *The Dark Fire* (No. 117), and
               The Hunter (No. 118).

The Talbot Press :
  Joseph Plunkett, *Collected Poems* (No. 135).

Messrs. T. Fisher Unwin, Ltd.:
  W. B. Yeats, *Poems* (Nos. 82, 126, 127).

Mr. J. G. Wilson :
  M. Caron Rock, *Or in the Grass* (No. 136).

The Poetry Bookshop (through Mr. Harold Monro) :
  Charlotte Mew, *The Farmer's Bride* (No. 123).
  H. Monro, *Children of Love* (No. 72), and
           Strange Meetings (No. 100).
  T. P. Cameron Wilson, *Magpies in Picardy* (No. 125).

No. 66 is an early version of a poem by Mr. Herbert Trench
appearing in the third edition of his *Poems with Fables in Prose*
(Constable & Co. Ltd.)

The Editor of *The Westminster Gazette* courteously confirmed the
authors' permissions in respect of Nos. 32, 80, and 94; and the
Editor of *The Spectator* gave permission in respect of No. 8.

₊ *These Biographical Notes are included in the cloth edition of "Poems of To-Day, Second Series," but not in the special school edition issued in stiff paper wrappers.*

BIOGRAPHICAL NOTES

(Revised to May, 1936)

A. E.

A. E.   *See* Russell, G. W.

ASQUITH

ASQUITH, HERBERT (1881), educated at Winchester and Balliol College, Oxford, is the second son of the former Prime Minister. He was called to the bar in 1907, but during the war served in France and Flanders from 1915 to 1918 as a captain in the R.F.A.   His poems are collected in *Poems 1912–1933* (1934), and his novels are *Wind's End* (1924), *Young Orland* (1927), and *Roon* (1929).

BARING

BARING, HON. MAURICE, O.B.E. (1874), was educated at Eton and Trinity College, Cambridge. He has been attaché at the British Embassies in Paris, Rome, and elsewhere, and was correspondent for the *Morning Post* in Manchuria 1904, special correspondent in Russia, and for *The Times* at Constantinople and in the Balkans. He was gazetted temporary lieutenant in the B.E.F. 1914 and held various appointments in the Air Force. Among his works are : *The Black Prince and other Poems* (1902), *Gaston de Foix and other Plays* (1903), *Desiderio* (1906), *Sonnets and Short Poems* (1906), *Collected Poems* (1911), *What I saw in Russia* (1913), *Mainsprings of Russia* (1914), *Outline of Russian Literature* (1915), *In Memoriam* (1917), *Poems 1914–1919* (1920), *Passing By* (1921) ; also novels, *Tinker's Leave* (1927), *The Coat without Seam* (1928).

BELLOC

BELLOC, JOSEPH HILAIRE PIERRE (1870), the son of a French father and English mother, was educated at the Oratory School, Edgbaston, received a French military training, and went to Balliol College, Oxford. His works include novels, essays, travel books, and historical studies, as well as poems, and he has contributed to various periodicals. His poems were published in *Verses and Sonnets* (1896), and in collected form in *Verses* (1910).   *The Bad Child's Book of Beasts* appeared in 1896, *More Beasts for Worse Children* in 1897, and *New Cautionary Tales* in 1930. The poem selected appeared in the *Westminster Gazette*.

BINYON

BINYON, ROBERT LAURENCE (1869), was educated at St. Paul's School and Trinity College, Oxford. He won the Newdigate Prize and contributed to *Primavera : Poems by Four Authors* (1890). From 1893 he was upon the staff of the British Museum and was long in charge of the Oriental Prints and Drawings. He has published prose works upon art and literature, a verse tragedy, *Attila* (1907), and various volumes of verse. *Lyric Poems* appeared in 1894, *London Visions* in 1896 and 1898 and the revised edition in 1908, *England and Other Poems* in 1909. His *Collected Poems* appeared in 1931.

BLUNDEN

BLUNDEN, EDMUND C. (1896), was educated at Christ's Hospital and Queen's College, Oxford. During the war he served as lieutenant in the 11th (Service) Batt. of the Royal Sussex Regiment. In 1916 he published three volumes of verse, *The Barn*, *Three Poems*, and *Pastorals*, and in 1920 *The Waggoner*, which contains the poems here selected. He has also edited, with Alan Porter, the poems of *John Clare* (1920). A collected edition of his *Poems* was issued in 1930.

BOAS

BOAS, FREDERICK S. (1862), was educated at Clifton College and Balliol College, Oxford. He was formerly a Professor of English Literature at Queen's College, Belfast, and Clark Lecturer in English Literature at Trinity College, Cambridge. Since 1905 he has been an Inspector of Higher Education in the L.C.C. Education Department. He is a Vice-President of the English Association and an Hon. LL.D. of St. Andrews. As a literary critic he has interested himself especially in Elizabethan drama and has edited the works of various authors of the sixteenth and seventeenth centuries. The poem selected is from a volume of verse, *Songs of Ulster and Balliol* (1917).

BOOTH

BOOTH, EVA GORE-, has published many volumes. Among these are : *Poems* (1898), *The One and the Many* (1904), *The Three Resurrections* (1905), *The Egyptian Pillar* (1907), *The Sorrowful Princess* (1907), *The Agate Lamp* (1912), *The Perilous Light* (1915), *The Death of Fionavar* (1916), *The Sword of Justice* (1918), *Broken Glory* (1918).

BOTTOMLEY

BOTTOMLEY, GORDON (1874), educated at the Grammar School, Keighley, is a poet and writer of verse plays. Among his volumes of verse are *The Gate of Smaragdus* (1904), *A Vision of Giorgione* (1910),

Chambers of Imagery, 1st Series (1907), 2nd Series (1912), the latter volume containing the poems selected. Five of his verse plays have been reissued in a volume published in 1920, containing *King Lear's Wife* (1915), *The Crier by Night* (1902), *The Riding to Lithend* (1909), *Midsummer Eve* (1905), *Laodice and Danaë* (1909). His later volumes are *Gruach and Britain's Daughter* : two verse plays (1921), *Poems of Thirty Years* (1925), and *Scenes and Plays* (1929).

BOURDILLON

BOURDILLON, FRANCIS WILLIAM (1852–1921), was educated at Haileybury and at Worcester College, Oxford. His chief works are : *Among the Flowers* (1878), a translation of *Aucassin and Nicolette* (1879), *Ailes d'Alouette* (1890), *A Lost God* (1891), *Sursum Corda* (1893), *Nephele* (1896), *Minuscula* (1897), *Through the Gateway* (1902), *Preludes and Romances* (1908).

BRIDGES

BRIDGES, ROBERT (1844–1931). Educated at Eton and Corpus Christi College, Oxford. Qualified in medicine. Poet Laureate, 1913. His published works consist of poems, plays and critical essays, and include *Milton's Prosody* (1891), *October* (1920), *New Verse* (1926). His last work, *The Testament of Beauty* (1929), has been widely read and highly praised.

BROOKE

BROOKE, RUPERT CHAWNER (1887–1915), was educated at Rugby, where his father was a house-master, and at King's College, Cambridge. After taking his degree he lived for a time at Grantchester. With others he was concerned in the publication of *Georgian Poetry* (1911–12), and of *New Numbers* (1914). In 1913 he travelled in America, Samoa, and Tahiti. He obtained a commission in the Royal Naval Division in 1914, and was sent to Antwerp. In 1915 he was sent to the Dardanelles, but became ill on the way and died at Scyros on April 23rd. His first volume, *Poems*, appeared in 1911, and the second, *1914 and Other Poems*, in 1915 after his death. A collected edition with a memoir was published in 1918. *Letters from America*, with a preface by Henry James, was published in 1916, as also his critical study, *John Webster and the Elizabethan Drama*.

BROWN

BROWN, THOMAS EDWARD (1830–1897), was born at Douglas, Isle of Man, and educated at King William's College in the island and at Christ Church, Oxford. He was successively Fellow of Oriel, Vice-Principal of King William's College, Headmaster of the Crypt School, Gloucester (where W. E. Henley was his pupil), and then for twenty-eight years a master at Clifton College. He retired in 1892 to his native island.   Most of his poetry was written at Clifton, but he was best known in his lifetime by his narrative poems in Manx dialect, *Fo'c's'le Yarns*, of which *Betsy Lee*, the first, appeared in 1873.   His *Collected Poems* were published posthumously in 1900 and *Selected Poems* in the Golden Treasury Series in 1908.

BULLEN

BULLEN, ARTHUR HENRY (1857–1920), was educated at the City of London School and Worcester College, Oxford.   He edited various Elizabethan plays and poems, and in 1887 published *Lyrics from the Song Books of the Elizabethan Age*, followed by a second series in 1888.   After his death a volume of his poems was published, *Weeping-Cross and Other Rimes*, which contains the poems selected.

CHAMBERS

CHAMBERS, EDMUND KERCHEVER, C.B. (1866), was born in Berkshire, and was educated at Marlborough and Corpus Christi College, Oxford.   He became Second Secretary of the Board of Education. He is the author of many critical works, dealing especially with the early history of the stage ; of these the most comprehensive is *The Mediaeval Stage* (1903).   A volume of his poems was printed for private circulation.

CHESTERTON

CHESTERTON, GILBERT KEITH (1874), was born in Kensington, was educated at St. Paul's School, and studied for a time at the Slade School of Art.   He is an essayist and writer upon literary and social subjects, a novelist, poet, and the author of a play, *Magic* (1913). His verse includes the book of satirical nonsense rhymes *Greybeards at Play* (1900), *The Wild Knight and Other Poems* (1900), *The Ballad of the White Horse* (1911), *Poems* (1915), and *Wine, Water, and Song* (1915), which contains the songs from his novel *The Flying Inn*. *Collected Poems* appeared in 1927.

COLUM

COLUM, PADRAIC (1881), born at Longford, is a writer of lyric verses and of plays, and has also written stories, sketches, and prose introductions to various books of selections.   His plays written for the Irish National Theatre include *The Land* (1905), *The Fiddler's House* (1907) recast from the earlier *Broken Soil*, and *Thomas Muskerry* (1910).   He contributed poems to a volume of lyric selections, *New Songs*, published by " A.E." in 1904, and published in 1907 a book of verse, *Wild Earth*, which has since been republished with additional poems.   He also contributed to *The Eyes of Youth* (1910).   Later volumes include *Creatures* (1927) and *A Half Day's Ride* (1932).

CREWE

CREWE, MARQUESS OF (ROBERT OFFLEY ASHBURTON CREWE-MILNES), K.G., P.C. (1858), was educated at Harrow and Trinity College, Cambridge. He has held various state offices, was President of the Board of Education in 1916 and Chairman of the London County Council in 1917. He has written political and literary articles and has 'published a volume of poetry, *Stray Verses, 1889–1890* (1891).

DEARMER

DEARMER, GEOFFREY (1893), was educated at Westminster and Christ Church, Oxford. He served from 1914 to 1919 in Gallipoli, Egypt, France, and England. His book, *Poems*, was published in 1918.

DE LA MARE

DE LA MARE, WALTER JOHN (1873), is a writer of verse and of prose romances. Some of his earlier poems appeared in the *Monthly Review*, 1902 to 1904, and in 1902 was published his first volume of verse, *Songs of Childhood*, under the pseudonym, Walter Ramal ; this has been re-edited (1916). In 1904 appeared *Henry Brocken*, a romance, and in 1906 *Poems*. *The Listeners* was published in 1912, *Peacock Pie* in 1913, *Motley* in 1918, a Collected Edition, *Poems 1901–1918*, in 1920, and *The Veil* in 1921. *The Return*, a novel (to which was awarded the first Prince Edmond de Polignac prize), and *The Three Mulla Mulgars*, a story for children, appeared in 1910, *A Child's Day* in 1912, *Stuff and Nonsense* in 1927, and many other volumes subsequently.

DRINKWATER

DRINKWATER, JOHN (1882), was educated at the Oxford High School and was for a time in various assurance offices. He has written critical prose, plays, and poems and is a contributor to several periodicals. His prose includes introductions to several volumes in " The Muses' Library " and " Everyman's Library," critical studies of William Morris (1912) and of Swinburne (1913), an essay, *The Lyric* (1915), and *Prose Papers* (1917). He was a co-founder of The Pilgrim Players, which developed into the Birmingham Repertory Theatre, and has written and produced plays, including *Abraham Lincoln* (1918), *Mary Stuart* (1921), and *Oliver Cromwell* (1921). His first book of verse was published at the age of twenty-one, and was followed by *The Death of Leander* (1906) and other volumes. *Poems 1908–1914* (1917) contains the author's own selection from his earlier work. *Collected Poems* appeared in 1923, and other volumes of poems and plays have been published since.

EDMINSON

EDMINSON, V. L., was a student of Newnham College, Cambridge, 1911–14, and later was English Lecturer at Salisbury Training College. The poem selected was published in the *Westminster Gazette*.

FIELD

FIELD, MICHAEL. The poems and plays published under this name are the work of an aunt and niece, Katharine Harris Bradley, who died in 1914, and Edith Emma Cooper, who died in 1913. The collaboration was so complete that no discrepancy can be detected. They wrote many plays, among them the following : *Callirrhoë, Fair Rosamund* (1884), *Stephania* (1892), *A Question of Memory* (1893), *Attila, My Attila* (1896), *Borgia* (1905), *Queen Mariamne* (1908), *The Tragedy of Pardon and Diane* (1911). Among their volumes of poetry are : *Underneath the Bough* (1893), *Poems of Adoration* (1912), *Mystic Trees* (1913), *In the Name of Time* (1919).

FLECKER

FLECKER, JAMES ELROY (1884–1915), was educated at Dean Close School, Cheltenham, of which his father was head-master, and at Uppingham and Trinity College, Oxford. He studied Oriental languages at Cambridge, and in 1910 went to Constantinople in the Consular Service. The rest of his life was spent mainly in the East with intervals in England. In March 1913 he was obliged by his health to go to Switzerland, and died of consumption at Davos on January 3rd, 1915. His first volume of verse, *The Bridge of Fire*, was published in 1907, and other volumes followed. A collected edition of his poems was published in 1916, with a biographical account by the editor, J. C. Squire, and of his prose in 1920.

FREEMAN

FREEMAN, JOHN (1880–1929). Born in London. Poet, critic, novelist. Winner of the Hawthornden Prize (1920). Chief executive officer in the Department of National Health Insurance. His published works include *Memories of Childhood and Other Poems* (1919), *Lyrical and Narrative Poems* (1921), *Prince Absalom* (1925), *Solomon and Balkis* (1926), *Collected Poems* (1928).

FURSE

FURSE, MARGARET CECILIA, is the daughter of Sir Henry Newbolt. Her book of poems, *The Gift*, was published in 1919.

GALSWORTHY

GALSWORTHY, JOHN (1869–1933). O.M., 1929. Educated at Harrow and New College, Oxford. Wrote a number of novels, plays, essays and short stories. His volumes of verse include *Moods, Songs and Doggerels* (1912) and *Verses New and Old* (1926).

GIBSON

GIBSON, WILFRID WILSON (1878), is a poet and writer of verse plays. His earliest published volumes are *Urlyn the Harper* (1900) and *The Queen's Vigil* (1902). Among the later volumes are *Daily Bread* (1910), *Fires* (1912), *Thoroughfares* (1914), *Borderlands* (1914), *Battle* (1915), *Friends* (1916), *Livelihood* (1917), *Whin* (1918), *Home* (1920), *Neighbours* (1920).

GRENFELL

GRENFELL, HON. JULIAN HENRY FRANCIS, D.S.O. (1888–1915), eldest son of the first Baron Desborough, was educated at Eton and Balliol College, Oxford. In 1910 he obtained a Commission in the Royal Dragoons and was stationed first in India and afterwards in S. Africa, but on the outbreak of the war was sent with his regiment to France, where he died from wounds in May 1915. The poem " Into Battle " was sent home in a letter dated " Flanders, April 1915."

HARDY

HARDY, THOMAS (1840–1929). O.M., 1910. Born in Dorset. An architect until 1887. Poet and novelist. His novels include *Far from the Madding Crowd* (1874), *Tess of the d'Urbervilles* (1891), *Jude the Obscure* (1895), and among his volumes of poems are *Wessex Poems* (1898), *Time's Laughing Stocks* (1909), *Satires of Circumstance* (1914), *Moments of Vision* (1917), and *Collected Poems* (1923).

HARVEY

HARVEY, FREDERICK WILLIAM (1888), was born in Gloucestershire. He was educated at Rossall and became a solicitor in 1912. He enlisted in August 1914, won the D.C.M. and obtained a commission in 1915. He was taken prisoner in 1916. He has published four volumes of verse : *A Gloucestershire Lad at Home and Abroad* (1916), *Gloucestershire Friends* (1917), *Ducks* (1919), and *Farewell* (1921). In *Comrades in Captivity* (1920) he gives a record of life in seven German prison camps.

HODGSON

HODGSON, RALPH (1871), is a poet whose first volume, *The Last Blackbird and other Lines*, appeared in 1907. Many of his poems were published in " The Flying Fame Booklets " (1913) : *Eve and Other Poems, The Bull, The Song of Honour, The Mystery and Other Poems* : some appeared in the form of broad-sheets of " The Flying Fame." A collected edition was published in 1917.

HODGSON

HODGSON, WILLIAM NOEL (1893–1916), was educated at Durham and at Christ Church, Oxford. He was given a commission in the Devon Regiment on the outbreak of war and fell in the battle of the Somme. His writings have been collected in a volume *Verse and Prose in Peace and War*, published in 1916.

HOUSMAN

HOUSMAN, ALFRED EDWARD (1859–1936), was educated at Broms-grove School and St. John's College, Oxford, of which he became an Honorary Fellow. He was Professor of Latin at University College, London, 1892–1911, and from 1911 Professor of Latin at Cambridge and Fellow of Trinity. His chief works are *A Shropshire Lad* (1896), *Last Poems* (1922), and editions of Manilius and Juvenal. He has contributed many papers to the *Journal of Philology*, the *Classical Review*, and the *Classical Quarterly*.

HUXLEY

HUXLEY, ALDOUS LEONARD (1894), was born at Godalming and educated at Eton and Balliol College, Oxford, taking a First Class in the School of English Language and Literature. He was on the Editorial Staff of the *Athenaeum* from 1919 to 1921, dramatic critic of the *Westminster Gazette* 1920–1, and is a contributor to various other periodicals. His publications in verse include *The Burning Wheel* (1916), *The Defeat of Youth* (1918), *Leda* (1920), and in prose *Limbo* (1920), *Crome Yellow* (1921).

JACOB

JACOB, VIOLET (VIOLET KENNEDY ERSKINE), is the author of a number of works in prose and verse. *The Sheep Stealers* (1902) and *The Interloper* (1904) are among her best-known novels. Her publications in verse include *Songs of Angus* (1915), *More Songs of Angus* (1918), *Bonnie Joann* (1921), and *The Northern Lights* (1927).

L. W.

L. W. *See* Whitmell.

LEDWIDGE

LEDWIDGE, FRANCIS (1892–1917), was a young Irish soldier-poet who fell in the war. He was discovered and encouraged by Lord Dunsany, who has edited his *Complete Poems*. His published works are : *Songs of the Fields* (1916), *Songs of Peace* (1917), *Last Songs* (1918), *Complete Poems* (1919).

LETTS

LETTS, WINIFRED M., was educated at St. Anne's, Abbots Bromley, and the Alexandra College, Dublin. Since 1916 she has been a masseuse in military and pensions hospitals. She is the author of several children's books, three novels, and two plays which were produced at the Abbey Theatre, Dublin. Her volumes of verse are *Songs from Leinster* (1913) and *Hallow E'en* (1916).

LYSAGHT

LYSAGHT, SIDNEY ROYSE (1857), is the author of several novels and of two volumes of verse, *Poems of the Unknown Way* (1901) and *Horizons and Landmarks* (1911).

MACAULAY

MACAULAY, ROSE, is a novelist who has also published two volumes of verse, *The Two Blind Countries* (1914) and *Three Days* (1919). The poem here selected appeared in the first number of the *Monthly Chapbook* (July 1919).

MACGREGOR

MACGREGOR, ALASDAIR ALPIN (1898), is the elder son of Colonel John MacGregor, I.M.S. He served in the Seaforth Highlanders from 1915 to 1919, was divisional guide during the third battle of Ypres, and was mentioned in dispatches twice. He has published articles in various papers, and is now a student in the Department of Economics at Edinburgh University.

MACKINTOSH

MACKINTOSH, EWART ALAN, M.C. (1893–1917), was educated at St. Paul's School and Christ Church, Oxford. Early in 1915 he received a commission in the Seaforth Highlanders, was sent to France, and was wounded and gassed at High Wood in August 1916. For a time he was at Cambridge as bombing instructor, but returned to France in October 1917 and fell in action the following November. He published a volume of poems, *A Highland Regiment*, in 1917, which contains the poem selected, and a second volume, *War, The Liberator*, was published after his death in 1918.

MASEFIELD

MASEFIELD, JOHN (1874), Poet Laureate since 1930. O.M., 1934. Poet, novelist, dramatist, and critic. His early volumes included *Salt Water Ballads* (1902) and tales of the sea. His plays *The Tragedy of Nan* (1908) and *Pompey the Great* (1910) were followed in 1911 by the Home University Library volume on *Shakespeare* and the first of his long narrative poems *The Everlasting Mercy*. *The*

Widow in the Bye Street succeeded in 1912, *Reynard the Fox* in 1919. *Collected Poems* appeared in 1923 (enlarged 1932). His novels include *Captain Margaret* (1908), *Multitude and Solitude* (1909), *Sard Harker* (1924), *Odtaa* (1926), and later tales of sea adventure. *Gallipoli* (1916) is a short history of the Dardanelles campaign of 1915.

MAYOR

MAYOR, BEATRICE (BEATRICE MEINERTZHAGEN), educated at home and in Paris, is the authoress of a volume of verse, *Poems*, published in 1919, and also of several plays.

MEW

MEW, CHARLOTTE, published in 1916 a volume of poems called *The Farmer's Bride*, from which the poem selected is taken.

MEYNELL

MEYNELL, ALICE (1850–1922). In her youth spent much time in Italy. Her published works include *The Rhythm of Life* (1893), *The Colour of Life* (1896), and *Poems*, complete edition (1923).

MONRO

MONRO, HAROLD (1879–1932). Born in Brussels. Educated at Radley and Caius College, Cambridge. In 1911 founded the *Poetry Review* and afterwards Poetry and Drama in conjunction with the Poetry Society. Founded the Poetry Bookshop in London in 1912. His published works include *Judas* (1908), *Before Dawn* (1910), *Children of Love* (1914), *Trees* (1915), *Strange Meetings* (1917), *Real Property* (1922), and *The Earth for Sale* (1928).

MOORE

MOORE, T. STURGE (1870), born at Hastings, is a wood-engraver and designer of book-plates and book covers, as well as a poet and prose writer. In 1920 he received a civil pension. He is a contributor to various periodicals, has written critical works on Dürer, Correggio, Altdorfer, Flaubert, and Blake, and has published plays in verse and several volumes of poems. His works include *The Vine Dresser* (1899), *The Gazelles* (1904), *Poems* (1906), *The Sea is Kind* (1914), *The Little School* (1905 and 1917), which contains the poems selected, *Danaë aforetime Blind Thamyris* (1920), *Tragic Mothers* (1920), and *The Powers of the Air* (1920).

MOORMAN

MOORMAN, FREDERIC WILLIAM (1872–1919), was born at Ashburton and educated at the school for the sons of Congregational ministers at Caterham, University College, London, University College, Aberystwyth, and Strasbourg. He became Lecturer in English at Aberystwyth in 1895 and at the Yorkshire College, Leeds, in 1898. Later he was appointed Professor of the English language at Leeds University. He was drowned when bathing near Litton-dale. His best-known critical work is *Robert Herrick : a Biography and Critical Study* (1910), which was followed by an edition of Herrick's poems in 1915. His enthusiasm for the Yorkshire dales was shown not only by his labours for the Yorkshire Dialect Society, but also by a number of original works in dialect, *Songs of the Ridings, Plays of the Ridings, Tales of the Ridings.*

MURRAY

MURRAY, GEORGE GILBERT AIMÉ (1866), was born at Sydney. He was educated at Merchant Taylors' School and St. John's College, Oxford. He was Professor of Greek at Glasgow University from 1889 to 1899 and has been Regius Professor of Greek at Oxford since 1908. He is Vice-Chairman of the Executive of the League of Nations Union. His publications include many critical works, among them *The Rise of the Greek Epic* (1907), *Four Stages of Greek Religion* (1912), as well as verse translations of plays by Aeschylus, Sophocles, Aristophanes, and more especially Euripides.

NEWBOLT

NEWBOLT, HENRY JOHN (1862), knighted 1915, was born at Bilston, Staffordshire, educated at Clifton College and Corpus Christi College, Oxford, and called to the Bar in 1887, but ceased to practise in 1899. From 1900 to 1904 he edited the *Monthly Review*. His writings consist of poems, plays, and novels ; he has edited anthologies and other works, and has published *A New Study of English Poetry* (1917). *Aladore*, a prose romance, appeared in 1914. The poems of the early volumes, *Admirals All* (1897), *The Island Race* (1898), *The Sailing of the Long Ships* (1902), and of other later volumes were published in collected form as *Poems New and Old* (1912), and again under the same title in a second edition (1919) which contains all the published verse from 1897 to 1918.

NICHOLS

NICHOLS, ROBERT MALISE BOWYER (1893), the son of J. B. B. Nichols (q.v. *Poems of To-day*, 1st Series), was educated at Win-chester and Trinity College, Oxford. He served in France as lieutenant in the R.F.A. in 1915, and was sent to America on propaganda work, 1918–19. He now holds the post of Professor of English Literature at Imperial College, Tokio, in succession to Lafcadio Hearn. His first volume of verse, *Invocation*, was published in 1916, *Ardours and Endurances* (which contains the poems selected) in 1917, *The Budded Branch* in 1918, and *Aurelia* in 1920.   *The Smile of the Sphinx* (prose) appeared in 1920.   He is a contributor to the *London Mercury* and other periodicals.

NIGHTINGALE

NIGHTINGALE, MADELEINE, is the elder daughter of Sir John Thrift.   She was married in 1908 to Charles Nightingale, the artist who has, either in black and white, woodcut, or water-colour, illustrated all her books.   She has published *The Babe's Book of Verse* (1918), *Verses Wise and Otherwise* (1918), *Pipes of Pan* (1918), *Nursery Lays* (1919), *Tony o' Dreams* (prose) (1919), *Tinker Tailor : Ballads and Rhymes* (1920), *Farmyard Ditties* (1920), *Ring a Ring o' Fairies* (1921).

O'NEILL

O'NEILL, MOIRA, has published two volumes of verse, *Songs of the Glens of Antrim* (1900) and *More Songs of the Glens of Antrim* (1921), as well as novels and tales.

O'SULLIVAN

O'SULLIVAN, SEUMAS, has published various volumes of prose sketches and verse.   The latter include : *The Twilight People* (1905), *Verses, Sacred and Profane* (1908), *Poems* (1912), *Epilogue to Praise of Angus* (1914), *The Rosses and other Poems* (1918).

PLUNKETT

PLUNKETT, JOSEPH MARY (1887–1916), the son of Count and Countess Plunkett, was born in Dublin and educated at the Roman Catholic University School, Belvedere College, and Stonyhurst.   He was a man of very wide reading, especially in scholastic philosophy and mysticism, and a great traveller.   He was interested in the *Irish Review* and in 1913 became its editor, and he was one of the three who inaugurated the Irish Theatre.   He published the *Circle and the Sword* in 1911.   His *Collected Poems* were edited by his sister, Geraldine Plunkett, in 1916.

ROCK

ROCK, MADELEINE CARON, published in 1915 a volume of verse called *Or in the Grass*.

RUSSELL

RUSSELL, GEORGE WILLIAM (1867–1935), better known under his pseudonym of " A. E.," was born in Lurgan, Co. Armagh, went to Dublin as a child, and was educated at a school in Rathmines.

He studied at the School of Art, where he became acquainted with the poet, W. B. Yeats. He was for a time an accountant, but later helped to organise co-operative societies and agricultural banks for the Irish Agricultural Organisation Society, of which he became assistant secretary, and editor of its official organ. He was an enthusiastic supporter of Irish Nationalism, an idealist and mystic, a writer of both prose and poetry, and a painter. He was one of the promoters of the Irish Literary Theatre in 1899. His first volume of poetry was *Homeward Songs by the Way* (1894), and this was followed by *The Earth Breath* (1897) and many others. His poems were published in collected form in 1913. His prose includes various works upon Irish matters, essays, a prose drama *Deirdre* (1907) acted by the Irish National Dramatic Company in 1902, *The Hero in Man* (1909), and *The Candle of Vision* (1918).

SACKVILLE

SACKVILLE, LADY MARGARET, has published *Poems* (1901), *A Hymn to Dionysos* (1905), *Bertrud and other Dramatic Poems* (1911), *Lyrics* (1912), *Songs of Aphrodite* (1913), *The Pageant of War* (1916), *Selected Poems* (1919).

SASSOON

SASSOON, SIEGFRIED LORAINE, M.C. (1886), was educated at Marlborough, and Clare College, Cambridge. He served in the Sussex Yeomanry from August 4th, 1914, received a commission in the Royal Welch Fusiliers in 1915, and served in both France and Palestine from 1915 to 1918. He was literary editor of the *Daily Herald* in 1919. His published work includes *The Old Huntsman* (1917), *Counter-Attack* (1918), *The War Poems of Siegfried Sassoon* (1919), *The Heart's Journey* (1928).

SHANKS

SHANKS, EDWARD BUXTON (1892), was educated at Merchant Taylors' School and at Trinity College, Cambridge, where he was editor of the *Granta*. He was gazetted 2nd Lieutenant, 8th South Lancs. Regiment, in 1914, and was invalided home in 1915, after which he worked at the War Office (1915–18). He was the first winner of the Hawthornden Prize for Imaginative Literature in 1919, and an Assistant Editor of the *London Mercury*. Among his published works are : *Songs* (1915), *Poems* (1916), *Queen of China* (1919), *Old Indispensables* (1919), *People of the Ruins* (1920), *The Island of Youth and other Poems* (1921).

SORLEY

SORLEY, CHARLES HAMILTON (1895–1915), was the son of Professor Sorley of Cambridge. He went to Marlborough, and was elected to a scholarship at University College, Oxford. He was gazetted Second Lieutenant in the Seventh (Service) Battalion of the Suffolk Regiment in August 1914, Lieutenant in November, and Captain in the following August. He was killed in action in October 1915. His poems were edited by his father in 1916, and were published under the title of *Marlborough and other Poems*. A volume of his letters has also been published (1919).

SPRING-RICE

SPRING-RICE, CECIL ARTHUR (1859–1918), was educated at Eton and at Balliol College, Oxford. In 1882 he was a clerk in the Foreign Office, and then followed a long experience at the Embassies or Legations of Washington, Tokio, Berlin, Constantinople, Teheran, St. Petersburg, Stockholm. In 1914 he returned to America as Ambassador. In January 1918 he was superseded by Lord Reading. He went to Ottawa and died there of heart failure on February 14th, 1918. He received the K.C.M.G. in 1906 and G.C.M.G. in 1916. He has published *Songs from the Book of Jaffier* (1900), and *The Story of Valeh and Hadijeh* (prose), translated from the Persian by Mirza Mahomed and C. Spring-Rice (1906). His *Collected Poems* were edited with a biographical notice and appreciation by Bernard Holland (1920).

STEPHENS

STEPHENS, JAMES, has published many works both in prose and verse. His prose writings include : *The Crock of Gold* (1912), *The Charwoman's Daughter* (1912), *Here are Ladies* (1913), *The Demi-Gods* (1914), *Irish Fairy Tales* (1920). *Insurrections* (1909), *The Hill of Vision* (1912), *Green Branches* (1916), *Reincarnations* (1918), are volumes of verse. *Collected Poems* (1926) was followed by *Poems* (1931).

TENNANT

TENNANT, HON. EDWARD WYNDHAM (1897–1916), the elder son of the late Lord Glenconner, was educated at Winchester, but left at the age of seventeen to study German in Germany for the Diplomatic Service. When war broke out, he joined the Grenadier Guards, served one year in France, and was killed at the Battle of the Somme on September 22, 1916. "Home Thoughts in Laventie" was sent home in a letter to his mother and published in *Worple Flit* (1916).

THOMAS

THOMAS, PHILIP EDWARD (1878–1917), educated at St. Paul's School and Lincoln College, Oxford, was a critic and essayist, writing reviews for the *Daily Chronicle* and other papers. He served with the Artists' Rifles during the war and was killed in action in France, April 1917. His published work includes verse, critical studies, topographical descriptions, various anthologies, and a novel, *The Happy-go-Lucky Morgans* (1913). His verse first appeared under the name of " Edward Eastaway." *Poems* was published in 1917, *Last Poems* in 1918, and a collected edition of his verse in 1920, with an introduction by W. de la Mare.

THOMPSON

THOMPSON, FRANCIS JOSEPH (1857–1907), was born at Preston, Lancs., and educated at Ushaw College. He studied medicine at Owens College, but failed to pass his examination, and did not succeed in any of the other openings that his father suggested. In 1885 he came to London, having already begun to take opium, and there he lived in miserable poverty and ill-health. He was later befriended by Mr. and Mrs. Wilfrid Meynell, who recognised his literary genius and helped him to break off his opium habits and regain some measure of health for a time. After a period of literary productiveness his health again failed, and he died of consumption in London. His first volume of poems was published in 1893, *Sister Songs* in 1895, and *New Poems* in 1897. A selection of his poetry was published in 1908, and a collected edition in 1913. His prose writings consist mainly of essays and reviews, including an essay upon Shelley.

TRENCH

TRENCH, HERBERT (1865–1923). Born in County Cork. Educated at Haileybury and Keble College, Oxford. Fellow of All Souls. Assistant Director of Special Enquiries at the Board of Education until 1908. His published works include *Deirdre Wedded* (1900), *New Poems* (1907), *Lyrics and Narrative Poems* (1911), *Poems with Fables in Prose* (1918).

TURNER

TURNER, WALTER J. (1889), was born in China and educated at Scotch College, Melbourne, and privately in Munich and Vienna. During the war he obtained a commission in the R.G.A. He is a contributor to the *London Mercury* and the *New Statesman*. He has published several volumes of verse : *The Hunter* (1916), *The Dark Fire* (1918), *Paris and Helen* (1921), *In Time Like Glass* (1921).

UNDERHILL

UNDERHILL, EVELYN (MRS. STUART MOORE), has edited *The Cloud of Unknowing*, and, with Dr. Rabindranath Tagore, the *Poems of Kabir*. She has written, among other works, *Mysticism* (1911),

Immanence, a book of verses (1910), *The Mystic Way* (1913), *Practical Mysticism* (1919), *Theophanies*, a book of verses (1916), *Jacopone da Todi* (1919), *Essentials of Mysticism and other Essays* (1920).

WHITMELL

MRS. LUCY WHITMELL (L. W.) was the author of the poem " Christ in Flanders," which appeared in the *Spectator* of September 11th, 1915. Mrs. Whitmell died at Leeds on May 7th, 1917, after a long illness.

WILSON

WILSON, T. P. CAMERON, was killed in France in early manhood on March 23rd, 1918. He left his work as a schoolmaster to enlist in the Grenadier Guards. Later on he was commissioned in the Sherwood Foresters. His collected poems, *Magpies in Picardy* (1919), have been edited with an introduction by Harold Monro. He published one novel, *The Friendly Enemy*. His letters from France are to be published shortly. He was a well-known contributor to the *Saturday Westminster* under the pseudonym " Tipuca."

YEATS

YEATS, WILLIAM BUTLER (1865), was born at Sandymount, Dublin, educated at Godolphin School, Hammersmith, and Erasmus Smith School, Dublin, studied art for a time in Dublin, and from 1885 onwards contributed poems to various papers. His first volume of poems, *The Wanderings of Oisin*, was published in 1889, *The Countess Kathleen and Other Lyrics* in 1892, and *The Land of Heart's Desire* in 1894, the contents of the three being republished in 1899, and his plays were produced by the Irish Literary Theatre in 1899, and his plays were produced by the Irish National Theatre. He has also written prose tales and essays, and has edited the works of Blake. More recent volumes are *The Wild Swans at Coole* (Dublin 1917, London 1919), *Four Plays for Dancers* (1921), *Later Poems* (1923), *Selected Poems Lyrical and Dramatic* (1929), and others.

POEMS OF TO-DAY

SECOND SERIES

1. FAREWELL TO PLACE OF COMFORT

For the last time, maybe, upon the knoll
   I stand.   The eve is golden, languid, sad . . .
Day like a tragic actor plays his rôle
To the last whispered word, and falls gold-clad.
I, too, take leave of all I ever had.

They shall not say I went with heavy heart :
Heavy I am, but soon I shall be free ;
I love them all, but oh ! I now depart
A little sadly, strangely, fearfully,
As one who goes to try a Mystery.

The bell is sounding down in Dedham Vale :
Be still, O bell ! too often standing here
When all the air was tremulous, fine, and pale,
Thy golden note so calm, so still, so clear,
Out of my stony heart has struck a tear.

And now tears are not mine.   I have release
From all the former and the later pain ;
Like the mid-sea I rock in boundless peace,

Soothed by the charity of the deep sea rain. . . .
Calm rain ! Calm sea ! Calm found, long sought in
    vain.

O bronzen pines, evening of gold and blue,
Steep mellow slope, brimmed twilit pools below,
Hushed trees, still vale dissolving in the dew,
Farewell ! Farewell ! There is no more to do.
We have been happy.   Happy now I go.
                                        Robert Nichols.

2. CHA TILL MACCRUIMEIN

(Departure of the 4th Camerons)

THE pipes in the streets were playing bravely,
    The marching lads went by,
With merry hearts and voices singing
    My friends marched out to die ;
But I was hearing a lonely pibroch
    Out of an older war,
" Farewell, farewell, farewell, MacCrimmon,
    MacCrimmon comes no more."

And every lad in his heart was dreaming
    Of honour and wealth to come,
And honour and noble pride were calling
    To the tune of the pipes and drum ;
But I was hearing a woman singing
    On dark Dunvegan shore,
" In battle or peace, with wealth or honour,
    MacCrimmon comes no more."

And there in front of the men were marching,
  With feet that made no mark,
The grey old ghosts of the ancient fighters
  Come back again from the dark ;
And in front of them all MacCrimmon piping
  A weary tune and sore,
" On the gathering day, for ever and ever,
  MacCrimmon comes no more."

Ewart Alan Mackintosh.

3. BEFORE ACTION

BY all the glories of the day
    And the cool evening's benison,
By that last sunset touch that lay
  Upon the hills when day was done,
By beauty lavishly outpoured
    And blessings carelessly received,
    By all the days that I have lived,
Make me a soldier, Lord.

By all of all man's hopes and fears,
    And all the wonders poets sing,
The laughter of unclouded years,
    And every sad and lovely thing ;
By the romantic ages stored
    With high endeavour that was his,
    By all his mad catastrophes,
Make me a man, O Lord.

I, that on my familiar hill
    Saw with uncomprehending eyes

A hundred of Thy sunsets spill
   Their fresh and sanguine sacrifice,
Ere the sun swings his noonday sword
   Must say good-bye to all of this ;—
   By all delights that I shall miss,
Help me to die, O Lord.
               William Noel Hodgson.

4. INTO BATTLE

THE naked earth is warm with spring,
   And with green grass and bursting trees
Leans to the sun's gaze glorying,
   And quivers in the sunny breeze ;
And life is colour and warmth and light,
   And a striving evermore for these ;
And he is dead who will not fight ;
   And who dies fighting has increase.

The fighting man shall from the sun
   Take warmth, and life from the glowing earth ;
Speed with the light-foot winds to run,
   And with the trees to newer birth ;
And find, when fighting shall be done,
   Great rest, and fullness after dearth.

All the bright company of Heaven
   Hold him in their high comradeship,
The Dog-Star, and the Sisters Seven,
   Orion's Belt and sworded hip.

The woodland trees that stand together,
   They stand to him each one a friend ;
They gently speak in the windy weather ,
   They guide to valley and ridge's end.

The kestrel hovering by day,
   And the little owls that call by night,
Bid him be swift and keen as they,
   As keen of ear, as swift of sight.

The blackbird sings to him, " Brother, brother,
   If this be the last song you shall sing,
Sing well, for you may not sing another ;
   Brother, sing."

In dreary, doubtful, waiting hours,
   Before the brazen frenzy starts,
The horses show him nobler powers ;
   O patient eyes, courageous hearts !

And when the burning moment breaks,
   And all things else are out of mind,
And only joy of battle takes
   Him by the throat, and makes him blind

Through joy and blindness he shall know,
   Not caring much to know, that still
Nor lead nor steel shall reach him, so
   That it be not the Destined Will.

The thundering line of battle stands,
   And in the air death moans and sings ;

But Day shall clasp him with strong hands,
  And Night shall fold him in soft wings.
                              Julian Grenfell.

5. THE ASSAULT

THE beating of the guns grows louder.
    " *Not long, boys, now.*"
My heart burns whiter, fearfuller, prouder.
Hurricanes grow
As guns redouble their fire.
Through the shaken periscope peeping,
I glimpse their wire :
Black earth, fountains of earth rise, leaping,
Spouting like shocks of meeting waves,
Death's fountains are playing,
Shells like shrieking birds rush over ;
Crash and din rises higher.
A stream of lead raves
Over us from the left . . . (we safe under cover !)
Crash ! Reverberation ! Crash !
Acrid smoke billowing. Flash upon flash.
Black smoke drifting. The German line
Vanishes in confusion, smoke. Cries, and cry
Of our men, " *Gah, yer swine !*
Ye're for it," die
In a hurricane of shell.

One cry :
" *We're comin' soon ! look out !* "
There is opened hell
Over there ; fragments fly,

Rifles and bits of men whirled at the sky :
Dust, smoke, thunder ! A sudden bout
Of machine guns chattering . . .
And redoubled battering,
As if in fury at their daring ! . . .

No good staring.
Time soon now . . . home . . . house on a
    sunny hill . . .
Gone like a flickered page :
Time soon now . . . zero . . . will engage . . .

A sudden thrill—
" Fix bayonets ! "
Gods ! we have our fill
Of fear, hysteria, exultation, rage,
Rage to kill.

My heart burns hot, whiter and whiter,
Contracts tighter and tighter,
Until I stifle with the will
Long forged, now used
(Though utterly strained)—
O pounding heart,
Baffled, confused,
Heart panged, head singing, dizzily pained—
To do my part.

Blindness a moment. Sick.
There the men are !
Bayonets ready : click !
Time goes quick ;

A stumbled prayer . . . somehow a blazing star
In a blue night . . . where ?
Again prayer.
The tongue trips.   Start :
How's time ?   Soon now.   Two minutes or less.
The gun's fury mounting higher . . .
Their utmost. I lift a silent hand. Unseen I bless
Those hearts will follow me.
And beautifully,
Now beautifully my will grips,
Soul calm and round and filmed and white !
A shout : " Men, no such order as retire ! "

I nod.
The whistle's 'twixt my lips . . .
I catch
A wan, worn smile at me.
Dear men !
The pale wrist-watch . . .
The quiet hand ticks on amid the din.
The guns again
Rise to a last fury, to a rage, a lust :
Kill ! Pound ! Kill ! Pound ! Pound !
Now comes the thrust !
My part . . . dizziness . . . will . . . but trust
These men.   The great guns rise ;
Their fury seems to burst the earth and skies !

They lift.

Gather, heart, all thoughts that drift ;
Be steel, soul,

Compress thyself
Into a round, bright whole.
I cannot speak.

Time.   Time !

I hear my whistle shriek,
Between teeth set ;
I fling an arm up,
Scramble up the grime
Over the parapet !

I'm up.   Go on.
Something meets us.
Head down into the storm that greets us.

A wail.
Lights.   Blurr.
Gone.
On, on.   Lead.   Leăd.   Hail.
Spatter.   Whirr ! Whirr !
" *Toward that patch of brown ;*
Direction left."   Bullets a stream.
Devouring thought crying in a dream.
Men, crumpled, going down . . .
Go on.   Go.
Deafness.   Numbness.   The loudening tornado.
Bullets.   Mud.   Stumbling and skating.
My voice's strangled shout :
" *Steady pace, boys !* "
The still light : gladness.

" *Look, sir.   Look out !* "
Ha ! ha ! Bunched figures waiting.
Revolver levelled quick !
Flick !   Flick !
Red as blood.
Germans.   Germans.
Good !   O good !
Cool madness.   *Robert Nichols.*

6. WAR'S CATARACT

IN this red havoc of the patient earth,
    Though higher yet the tide of battle rise,
Now has the hero cast away disguise,
And out of ruin splendour comes to birth.
This is the field where Death and Honour meet,
And all the lesser company are low :
Pale Loveliness has left her mirror now
And walks the Court of Pain with silent feet.

From cliff to cliff war's cataract goes down,
Hurling its booming waters to the shock ;
And, tossing high their manes of gleaming spray,
The crested chargers leap from rock to rock,
While over all, dark though the thunder frown,
The rainbows climb above to meet the day.
                                Herbert Asquith.

7. FULFILMENT

WAS there love once ?   I have forgotten her.
        Was there grief once ?   Grief yet is mine.
Other loves I have, men rough, but men who stir
More grief, more joy, than love of thee and thine.

Faces cheerful, full of whimsical mirth,
Lined by the wind, burned by the sun ;
Bodies enraptured by the abounding earth,
As whose children we are brethren : one.

And any moment may descend hot death
To shatter limbs ! pulp, tear, blast
Beloved soldiers who love rough life and breath
Not less for dying faithful to the last.

O the fading eyes, the grimed face turned bony,
Oped mouth gushing, fallen head,
Lessening pressure of a hand shrunk, clammed, and
     stony !
O sudden spasm, release of the dead !

Was there love once ?   I have forgotten her.
Was there grief once ?   Grief yet is mine.
O loved, living, dying, heroic soldier,
All, all, my joy, my grief, my love, are thine !
                         Robert Nichols.

8. CHRIST IN FLANDERS

WE had forgotten You, or very nearly—
     You did not seem to touch us very nearly—
Of course we thought about You now and then ;
Especially in any time of trouble—
We knew that You were good in time of trouble—
     But we are very ordinary men.

And there were always other things to think of—
There's lots of things a man has got to think of—
    His work, his home, his pleasure, and his wife ;
And so we only thought of You on Sunday—
Sometimes, perhaps, not even on a Sunday—
    Because there's always lots to fill one's life.

And, all the while, in street or lane or byway—
In country lane, in city street, or byway—
    You walked among us, and we did not see.
Your feet were bleeding as You walked our pave-
    ments—
How *did* we miss Your footprints on our pavements ?—
    Can there be other folk as blind as we ?

Now we remember ; over here in Flanders—
(It isn't strange to think of You in Flanders)—
    This hideous warfare seems to make things clear.
We never thought about You much in England—
But now that we are far away from England,
    We have no doubts, we know that You are here.

You helped us pass the jest along the trenches—
Where, in cold blood, we waited in the trenches—
    You touched its ribaldry and made it fine.
You stood beside us in our pain and weakness—
We're glad to think You understand our weakness—
    Somehow it seems to help us not to whine.

We think about You kneeling in the Garden—
Ah ! God ! the agony of that dread Garden—
    We know You prayed for us upon the cross.

If anything could make us glad to bear it—
'Twould be the knowledge that You willed to bear it—
  Pain—death—the uttermost of human loss.

Though we forgot You—You will not forget us—
We feel so sure that You will not forget us—
  But stay with us until this dream is past.
And so we ask for courage, strength, and pardon—
Especially, I think, we ask for pardon—
  And that You'll stand beside us to the last.

Lucy Whitmell.

9. AT THE WARS

Now that I am ta'en away
    And may not see another day
What is it to my eye appears ?
What sound rings in my stricken ears ?
Not even the voice of any friend
Or eyes beloved-world-without-end,
But scenes and sounds of the country-side
In far England across the tide :
An upland field when spring's begun,
Mellow beneath the evening sun. . . .
A circle of loose and lichened wall
Over which seven red pines fall. . . .
An orchard of wizen blossoming trees
Wherein the nesting chaffinches
Begin again the self-same song
All the late April day-time long. . . .

Paths that lead a shelving course
Between the chalk scarp and the gorse
By English downs ; and oh ! too well
I hear the hidden, clanking bell
Of wandering sheep. . . . I see the brown
Twilight of the huge empty down. . . .
Soon blotted out ! for now a lane
Glitters with warmth of May-time rain,
And on a shooting briar I see
A yellow bird who sings to me.

O yellow-hammer, once I heard
Thy brief song when no other bird
Could to my sunk heart comfort bring ;
But now I would not have thee sing
So sharp thy note is with the pain
Of England I may not see again !
Yet sing thy song : there answereth
Deep in me a voice which saith :
   " The gorse upon the twilit down,
     The English loam so sunset brown,
     The bowed pines and the sheep-bells' clamour,
     The wet, lit lane and the yellow-hammer,
     The orchard and the chaffinch song
     Only to the Brave belong.
     And he shall lose their joy for aye
     If their price he cannot pay,
     Who shall find them dearer far
     Enriched by blood after long War."

Robert Nichols.

10. HOME THOUGHTS IN LAVENTIE

GREEN gardens in Laventie !
　　Soldiers only know the street
Where the mud is churned and splashed about
　　By battle-wending feet ;
And yet beside one stricken house there is a glimpse
　　of grass.
　　　　Look for it when you pass.

Beyond the church whose pitted spire
　　Seems balanced on a strand
Of swaying stone and tottering brick
　　Two roofless ruins stand,
And here behind the wreckage where the back wall
　　should have been
　　　　We found a garden green.

The grass was never trodden on,
　　The little path of gravel
Was overgrown with celandine,
　　No other folk did travel
Along its weedy surface, but the nimble-footed mouse
　　　　Running from house to house.

So all among the vivid blades
　　Of soft and tender grass
We lay, nor heard the limber wheels
　　That pass and ever pass
In noisy continuity until their very rattle
　　　　Seems in itself a battle.

At length we rose up from this ease
Of tranquil happy mind,
And searched the garden's little length
A fresh pleasaunce to find ;
And there some yellow daffodils and jasmine hanging
high
Did rest the tired eye.

The fairest and most fragrant
Of the many sweets we found,
Was a little bush of daphne flower
Upon a grassy mound,
And so thick were the blossoms set and so divine the
scent
That we were well content.

Hungry for spring, I bent my head,
The perfume fanned my face,
And all my soul was dancing
In that little lovely place,
Dancing with a measured step from wrecked and
shattered towns
Away upon the Downs.

I saw green banks of daffodil,
Slim poplars in the breeze,
Great tan-brown hares in gusty March
A-courting on the leas ;
And meadows with their glittering streams, and silver
scurrying dace,
Home—what a perfect place !

E. Wyndham Tennant.

11. BACK TO REST

A LEAPING wind from England,
　　The skies without a stain,
Clean cut against the morning,
　　Slim poplars after rain,
The foolish noise of sparrows
　　And starlings in a wood—
After the grime of battle
　　We know that these are good.

Death whining down from heaven,
　　Death roaring from the ground,
Death stinking in the nostril,
　　Death shrill in every sound,
Doubting we charged and conquered—
　　Hopeless we struck and stood.
Now when the fight is ended
　　We know that it was good.

We that have seen the strongest
　　Cry like a beaten child,
The sanest eyes unholy,
　　The cleanest hands defiled,
We that have known the heart-blood
　　Less than the lees of wine,
We that have seen men broken,
　　We know man is divine.

William Noel Hodgson.

12. OXFORD IN WAR-TIME

WHAT alters you, familiar lawn and tower,
　　Arched alley, and garden green to the grey wall
With crumbling crevice and the old wine-red flower,
Solitary in summer sun ? for all

Is like a dream : I tread on dreams !   No stir
Of footsteps, voices, laughter !   Even the chime
Of many-memoried bells is lonelier
In this neglected ghostliness of Time.

What stealing touch of separation numb
Absents you ?   Yet my heart springs up to adore
The shrining of your soul, that is become
Nearer and oh ! far dearer than before.

It is as if I looked on the still face
Of a Mother, musing where she sits alone.
She is with her sons, she is not in this place ;
She is gone out into far lands unknown.

Because that filled horizon occupies
Her heart with mute prayer and divining fear
Therefore her hands so calm lie, and her eyes
See nothing ; and men wonder at her here :

But far in France ; on the torn Flanders plain ;
By Sinai ; in the Macedonian snows ;
The fly-plagued sands of Tigris, heat and rain ;
On wandering water, where the black squall blows

Less danger than the bright wave ambushes,
She bears it out.   All the long day she bears,
And the sudden hour of instant challenges
To act, that searches all men, no man spares.

She is with her sons, leaving a virtue gone
Out of her sacred places : what she bred
Lives other life than this, that sits alone,
Though still in dream starrily visited !

For O in youth she lives, not in her age.
Her soul is with the springtime and the young ;
And she absents her from the learned page,
Studious of high histories yet unsung,

More passionately prized than wisdom's book
Because her own.   Her faith is in those eyes
That clear into the gape of hell can look,
Putting to proof ancient philosophies

Such as the virgin Muses would rehearse
Beside the silvery, swallow-haunted stream,
Under the grey towers.   But immortal verse
Is now exchanged for its immortal theme—

Victory ; proud loss ; and the enduring mind ;
Youth, that has passed all praises, and has won
More than renown, being that which faith divined
Reality more radiant than the sun.

She gave, she gives, more than all anchored days
Of dedicated lore, of storied art ;
And she resigns her beauty to men's gaze
To mask the riches of her bleeding heart.

Laurence Binyon.

13. THE NON-COMBATANT

AMONG a race high-handed, strong of heart,
    Sea-rovers, conquerors, builders in the waste,
He had his birth ; a nature too complete,
Eager and doubtful, no man's soldier sworn
And no man's chosen captain ; born to fail,
A name without an echo : yet he too
Within the cloister of his narrow days
Fulfilled the ancestral rites, and kept alive
The eternal fire ; it may be, not in vain ;
For out of those who dropped a downward glance
Upon the weakling huddled at his prayers,
Perchance some looked beyond him, and then first
Beheld the glory, and what shrine it filled,
And to what Spirit sacred : or perchance
Some heard him chanting, though but to himself,
The old heroic names : and went their way :
And hummed his music on the march to death.

Henry Newbolt.

14. EPITAPH ON AN ARMY OF MERCENARIES

THESE, in the day when Heaven was falling,
    The hour when Earth's foundation fled,
Followed their mercenary calling
    And took their wages and are dead.

Their shoulders held the sky suspended ;
  They stood, and Earth's foundations stay ;
What God abandoned, these defended
  And saved the sum of things for pay.
                          A. E. Housman.

15. THE VOLUNTEER

Here lies the clerk who half his life had spent
    Toiling at ledgers in a city grey,
Thinking that so his days would drift away
With no lance broken in life's tournament :
Yet ever 'twixt the books and his bright eyes
The gleaming eagles of the legions came,
And horsemen, charging under phantom skies,
Went thundering past beneath the oriflamme.

And now those waiting dreams are satisfied ;
From twilight to the halls of dawn he went ;
His lance is broken ; but he lies content
With that high hour, in which he lived and died.
And falling thus, he wants no recompense,
Who found his battle in the last resort ;
Nor needs he any hearse to bear him hence,
Who goes to join the men of Agincourt.
                          Herbert Asquith.

16. THE WAR FILMS

O living pictures of the dead,
    O songs without a sound,
O fellowship whose phantom tread
    Hallows a phantom ground—
How in a gleam have these revealed
    The faith we had not found.

We have sought God in a cloudy Heaven,
 We have passed by God on earth :
His seven sins and his sorrows seven,
 His wayworn mood and mirth,
Like a ragged cloak have hid from us
 The secret of his birth.

Brother of men, when now I see
 The lads go forth in line,
Thou knowest my heart is hungry in me
 As for thy bread and wine :
Thou knowest my heart is bowed in me
 To take their death for mine.

     Henry Newbolt.

17. THE UNRETURNING SPRING

A LEAF on the grey sand-path
 Fallen, and fair with rime !
A yellow leaf, a scarlet leaf,
And a green leaf ere its time.

Days rolled in blood, days torn,
Days innocent, days burnt black,
What is it the wind is sighing
As the leaves float, swift or slack ?

The year's pale spectre is crying
For beauty invisibly shed,
For the things that never were told
And were killed in the minds of the dead.

     Laurence Binyon.

18. HARROW AND FLANDERS

HERE in the marshland, past the battered bridge,
One of a hundred grains untimely sown,
Here, with his comrades of the hard-won ridge,
He rests, unknown.

His horoscope had seemed so plainly drawn—
School triumphs earned apace in work and play ;
Friendships at will ; then love's delightful dawn
And mellowing day ;

Home fostering hope ; some service to the State ;
Benignant age ; then the long tryst to keep
Where in the yew-tree shadow congregate
His fathers sleep.

Was here the one thing needful to distil
From life's alembic, through this holier fate,
The man's essential soul, the hero will ?
We ask ; and wait.

Lord Crewe.

19. IN MEMORIAM, A. H.

*(Auberon Herbert, Captain Lord Lucas, R.F.C., killed November 3rd,
1916)*

THE wind had blown away the rain
That all day long had soaked the level plain.
Against the horizon's fiery wrack,
The sheds loomed black.
And higher, in their tumultuous concourse met,
The streaming clouds, shot-riddled banners, wet

With the flickering storm,
Drifted and smouldered, warm
With flashes sent
From the lower firmament.
And they concealed—
They only here and there through rifts revealed
A hidden sanctuary of fire and light,
A city of chrysolite.

We looked and laughed and wondered, and I said :
That orange sea, those oriflammes outspread
Were like the fanciful imaginings
That the young painter flings
Upon the canvas bold,
Such as the sage and the old
Make mock at, saying it could never be ;
And you assented also, laughingly.
I wondered what they meant,
That flaming firmament,
Those clouds so grey so gold, so wet so warm,
So much of glory and so much of storm,
The end of the world, or the end
Of the war—remoter still to me and you, my friend.

Alas ! it meant not this, it meant not that :
It meant that now the last time you and I
Should look at the golden sky,
And the dark fields large and flat,
And smell the evening weather,
And laugh and talk and wonder both together.

The last, last time.   We nevermore should meet
In France or London street,
Or fields of home.   The desolated space
Of life shall nevermore
Be what it was before.
No one shall take your place.
No other face
Can fill that empty frame.
There is no answer when we call your name.
We cannot hear your step upon the stair.
We turn to speak and find a vacant chair.
Something is broken which we cannot mend.
God has done more than take away a friend
In taking you ; for all that we have left
Is bruised and irremediably bereft.
There is none like you.   Yet not that alone
Do we bemoan ;
But this ; that you were greater than the rest,
And better than the best.

O liberal heart fast-rooted to the soil,
O lover of ancient freedom and proud toil,
Friend of the gipsies and all wandering song,
The forest's nursling and the favoured child
Of woodlands wild—
O brother to the birds and all things free,
Captain of liberty !

Deep in your heart the restless seed was sown ;
The vagrant spirit fretted in your feet ;
We wondered could you tarry long,
And brook for long the cramping street,

Or would you one day sail for shores unknown,
And shake from you the dust of towns, and spurn
The crowded market-place—and not return ?
You found a sterner guide ;
You heard the guns.   Then, to their distant fire,
Your dreams were laid aside ;
And on that day, you cast your heart's desire
Upon a burning pyre ;
You gave your service to the exalted need,
Until at last from bondage freed,
At liberty to serve as you loved best,
You chose the noblest way.   God did the rest.

So when the spring of the world shall shrive our stain,
After the winter of war,
When the poor world awakes to peace once more,
After such night of ravage and of rain,
You shall not come again.
You shall not come to taste the old spring weather,
To gallop through the soft untrampled heather,
To bathe and bake your body on the grass.
We shall be there, alas !
But not with you.   When Spring shall wake the earth,
And quicken the scarred fields to the new birth,
Our grief shall grow.   For what can Spring renew
More fiercely for us than the need of you ?

That night I dreamt they sent for me and said
That you were missing, " missing, missing—dead " :
I cried when in the morning I awoke,
And all the world seemed shrouded in a cloak ;

But when I saw the sun,
And knew another day had just begun,
I brushed the dream away, and quite forgot
The nightmare's ugly blot.
So was the dream forgot. The dream came true.
Before the night I knew
That you had flown away into the air
For ever. Then I cheated my despair.
I said
That you were safe—or wounded—but not dead.
Alas ! I knew
Which was the false and true.

And after days of watching, days of lead,
There came the certain news that you were dead.
You had died fighting, fighting against odds,
Such as in war the gods
Aethereal dared when all the world was young ;
Such fighting as blind Homer never sung,
Nor Hector nor Achilles never knew,
High in the empty blue.

High, high, above the clouds, against the setting sun,
The fight was fought, and your great task was done.

Of all your brave adventures this the last
The bravest was and best ;
Meet ending to a long embattled past,
This swift, triumphant, fatal quest,
Crowned with the wreath that never perisheth,
And diadem of honourable death ;

Swift Death aflame with offering supreme
And mighty sacrifice,
More than all mortal dream ;
A soaring death, and near to Heaven's gate ;
Beneath the very walls of Paradise.
Surely with soul elate,
You heard the destined bullet as you flew,
And surely your prophetic spirit knew
That you had well deserved that shining fate.

Here is no waste,
No burning Might-have-been,
No bitter after-taste,
None to censure, none to screen,
Nothing awry, nor anything misspent ;
Only content, content beyond content,
Which hath not any room for betterment.

God, Who had made you valiant, strong and swift,
And maimed you with a bullet long ago,
And cleft your riotous ardour with a rift,
And checked your youth's tumultuous overflow,
Gave back your youth to you,
And packed in moments rare and few
Achievements manifold
And happiness untold,
And bade you spring to Death as to a bride,
In manhood's ripeness, power and pride,
And on your sandals the strong wings of youth.

He let you leave a name
To shine on the entablatures of truth,
For ever :
To sound for ever in answering halls of fame.

For you soared onwards to that world which rags
Of clouds, like tattered flags,
Concealed ; you reached the walls of chrysolite,
The mansions white ;
And losing all, you gained the civic crown
Of that eternal town,
Wherein you passed a rightful citizen
Of the bright commonwealth ablaze beyond our ken.

Surely you found companions meet for you
In that high place ;
You met there face to face
Those you had never known, but whom you knew :
Knights of the Table Round,
And all the very brave, the very true,
With chivalry crowned ;
The captains rare,
Courteous and brave beyond our human air ;
Those who had loved and suffered overmuch,
Now free from the world's touch.
And with them were the friends of yesterday,
Who went before and pointed you the way ;
And in that place of freshness, light and rest,

Where Lancelot and Tristram vigil keep
Over their King's long sleep,

Surely they made a place for you,
Their long-expected guest,
Among the chosen few,
And welcomed you, their brother and their friend,
To that companionship which hath no end.

And in the portals of the sacred hall
You hear the trumpet's call,
At dawn upon the silvery battlement,
Re-echo through the deep
And bid the sons of God to rise from sleep,
And with a shout to hail
The sunrise on the city of the Grail :
The music that proud Lucifer in Hell
Missed more than all the joys that he forwent.
You hear the solemn bell
At vespers, when the oriflammes are furled ;
And then you know that somewhere in the world,
That shines far-off beneath you like a gem,
They think of you, and when you think of them
You know that they will wipe away their tears,
And cast aside their fears ;
That they will have it so,
And in no otherwise ;
That it is well with them because they know,
With faithful eyes,
Fixed forward and turned upwards to the skies,
That it is well with you,
Among the chosen few,
Among the very brave, the very true.

                                        Maurice Baring.

20. LAMENT

WE who are left, how shall we look again
    Happily on the sun or feel the rain
Without remembering how they who went
Ungrudgingly and spent
Their lives for us loved, too, the sun and rain ?
A bird among the rain-wet lilac sings—
But we, how shall we turn to little things
And listen to the birds and winds and streams
Made holy by their dreams,
Nor feel the heart-break in the heart of things ?
                 Wilfrid Wilson Gibson.

21. THE DYING PATRIOT

DAY breaks on England down the Kentish hills,
    Singing in the silence of the meadow-footing rills,
Day of my dreams, O day !
    I saw them march from Dover, long ago,
    With a silver cross before them, singing low,
Monks of Rome from their home where the blue seas
        break in foam,
    Augustine with his feet of snow.

Noon strikes on England, noon on Oxford town,
—Beauty she was statue cold—there's blood upon her
        gown :
Noon of my dreams, O noon !
    Proud and godly kings had built her, long ago,
    With her towers and tombs and statues all arow,
With her fair and floral air and the love that lingers
        there,
    And the streets where the great men go.

Evening on the olden, the golden sea of Wales,
When the first star shivers and the last wave pales :
O evening dreams !
   There's a house that Britons walked in, long ago,
   Where now the springs of ocean fall and flow,
And the dead robed in red and sea-lilies overhead
   Sway when the long winds blow.

Sleep not, my country : though night is here, afar
Your children of the morning are clamorous for war :
Fire in the night, O dreams !
   Though she send you as she sent you, long ago,
   South to desert, east to ocean, west to snow,
West of these out to seas colder than the Hebrides
        I must go
   Where the fleet of stars is anchored and the young
        Star-captains glow.
                 J. E. Flecker.

22. MEN WHO MARCH AWAY

(Song of the Soldiers)

WHAT of the faith and fire within us
     Men who march away
  Ere the barn-cocks say
  Night is growing gray,
Leaving all that here can win us ;
What of the faith and fire within us
     Men who march away ?

Is it a purblind prank, O think you,
  Friend with the musing eye,
  Who watch us stepping by
  With doubt and dolorous sigh ?
Can much pondering so hoodwink you
Is it a purblind prank, O think you,
  Friend with the musing eye ?

Nay.   We well see what we are doing,
  Though some may not see—
  Dalliers as they be—
  England's need are we ;
Her distress would leave us rueing :
Nay.   We'll see what we are doing,
  Though some may not see.

In our heart of hearts believing
  Victory crowns the just,
  And that braggarts must
  Surely bite the dust,
Press we to the field ungrieving,
In our heart of hearts believing
  Victory crowns the just.

Hence the faith and fire within us
  Men who march away
  Ere the barn-cocks say
  Night is growing gray,
Leaving all that here can win us ;
Hence the faith and fire within us
  Men who march away.

Thomas Hardy.

September 5, 1914.

3—P.T.D. 2

23. ON BEHALF OF SOME IRISHMEN NOT FOLLOWERS OF TRADITION

THEY call us aliens, we are told,
    Because our wayward visions stray
From that dim banner they unfold,
The dreams of worn-out yesterday.
The sum of all the past is theirs,
The creeds, the deeds, the fame, the name,
Whose death-created glory flares
And dims the spark of living flame.
They weave the necromancer's spell,
And burst the graves where martyrs slept,
Their ancient story to retell,
Renewing tears the dead have wept.
And they would have us join their dirge,
This worship of an extinct fire
In which they drift beyond the verge
Where races all outworn expire.
The worship of the dead is not
A worship that our hearts allow,
Though every famous shade were wrought
With woven thorns above the brow.

We fling our answer back in scorn :
" We are less children of this clime
Than of some nation yet unborn
Or empire in the womb of time.
We hold the Ireland in the heart
More than the land our eyes have seen,
And love the goal for which we start
More than the tale of what has been."

The generations as they rise
May live the life men lived before,
Still hold the thought once held as wise,
Go in and out by the same door.
We leave the easy peace it brings :
The few we are shall still unite
In fealty to unseen kings
Or unimaginable light.
We would no Irish sign efface,
But yet our lips would gladlier hail
The firstborn of the Coming Race
Than the last splendour of the Gael.
No blazoned banner we unfold—
One charge alone we give to youth,
Against the sceptred myth to hold
The golden heresy of truth.

A. E.

24. I VOW TO THEE, MY COUNTRY

(Written January 12th, 1918, the last night which he spent at the
British Embassy at Washington, at the end of his service to England,
and hardly more than a month before his death.)

I vow to thee, my country—all earthly things
    above—
Entire and whole and perfect, the service of my love,
The love that asks no questions : the love that stands
    the test,
That lays upon the altar the dearest and the best :
The love that never falters, the love that pays the
    price,
The love that makes undaunted the final sacrifice.

And there's another country, I've heard of long ago—
Most dear to them that love her, most great to them
    that know—
We may not count her armies : we may not see her
    king—
Her fortress is a faithful heart, her pride is suffering—
And soul by soul and silently her shining bounds
    increase,
And her ways are ways of gentleness and all her paths
    are peace.

Cecil Spring-Rice.

25. HAPPY IS ENGLAND NOW

THERE is not anything more wonderful
    Than a great people moving towards the deep
Of an unguessed and unfeared future ; nor
Is aught so dear of all held dear before
As the new passion stirring in their veins
When the destroying Dragon wakes from sleep.

Happy is England now, as never yet !
And though the sorrows of the slow days fret
Her faithfullest children, grief itself is proud.
Ev'n the warm beauty of this spring and summer
That turns to bitterness turns then to gladness,
Since for this England the beloved ones died.

Happy is England in the brave that die
For wrongs not hers and wrongs so sternly hers ;

Happy in those that give, give, and endure
The pain that never the new years may cure ;
Happy in all her dark woods, green fields, towns,
Her hills and rivers and her chafing sea.

Whate'er was dear before is dearer now.
There's not a bird singing upon his bough
But sings the sweeter in our English ears :
There's not a nobleness of heart, hand, brain
But shines the purer ; happiest is England now
In those that fight, and watch with pride and tears.
John Freeman.

26. AVE, MATER—ATQUE VALE

THE deathless mother, grey and battle-scarred,
    Lies in the sanctuary of stately trees,
Where the deep Northern night is saffron starred
    Above her head, and thro' the dusk she sees
God's shadowy fortress keep unsleeping guard.

From her full breast we drank of joy and mirth
    And gave to her a boy's unreasoned heart,
Wherein Time's fullness was to bring to birth
    Such passionate allegiance that to part
Seemed like the passing of all light on earth.

Now on the threshold of a man's estate,
    With a new depth of love akin to pain
I ask thy blessing, while I dedicate
    My life and sword, with promise to maintain
Thine ancient honour yet inviolate.

Last night dream-hearted in the Abbey's spell
   We stood to sing old Simeon's passing hymn,
When sudden splendour of the sunset fell
   Full on my eyes, and passed and left all dim—
At once a summons and a deep farewell.

I am content—our life is but a trust
   From the great hand of God, and if I keep
The immortal Treasure clean of mortal rust
   Against His claim, 'tis well, and let me sleep
Among the not dishonourable dust.

                William Noel Hodgson.

27. THE SCRIBE

WHAT lovely things
      Thy hand hath made :
The smooth-plumed bird
In its emerald shade,
The seed of the grass,
The speck of stone
Which the wayfaring ant
Stirs—and hastes on !

Though I should sit
By some tarn in thy hills,
Using its ink
As the spirit wills
To write of Earth's wonders,
Its live, willed things,
Flit would the ages
On soundless wings

Ere unto Z
My pen drew nigh ;
Leviathan told,
And the honey-fly :
And still would remain
My wit to try—
My worn reeds broken,
The dark tarn dry,
All words forgotten—
Thou, Lord, and I.

Walter de la Mare.

28. WIND'S WORK

KATE rose up early as fresh as a lark,
    Almost in time to see vanish the dark ;
Jack rather later, bouncing from bed,
Saw fade on the dawn's cheek the last flush of red :
Yet who knows
When the wind rose ?

Kate went to watch the new lambs at their play
And stroke the white calf born yesterday ;
Jack sought the woods where trees grow tall
As who would learn to swarm them all :
Yet who knows
Where the wind goes ?

Kate has sown candy-tuft, lupins and peas,
Carnations, forget-me-not and heart's ease ;

Jack has sown cherry-pie, marigold,
Love-that-lies-bleeding and snap-dragons bold :
But who knows
What the wind sows ?

Kate knows a thing or two useful at home,
Darns like a fairy, and churns like a gnome ;
Jack is a wise man at shaping a stick,
Once he's in the saddle the pony may kick.
But hark to the wind how it blows !
None comes, none goes,
None reaps or mows,
No friends turn foes,
No hedge bears sloes,
And no cock crows,
But the wind knows !

T. Sturge Moore.

29. THE LAMP FLOWER

THE campion white
   Above the grass
Her lamps doth light
   Where fairies pass.

Softly they show
   The secret way,
Unflickering glow
   For elf and fay.

My little thought
   Hath donned her shoe,
And all untaught
   Gone dancing too.

Sadly I peer
   Among the grass
And seem to hear
   The fairies pass,

But where they go
   I cannot see,
Too faintly glow
   The lamps for me.

My thought is gone
   With fay and elf,
We mope alone,
   I and myself.

Margaret Cecilia Furse.

30. JULY FUGITIVE

CAN you tell me where has hid her,
   Pretty Maid July ?
I would swear one day ago
   She passed by,
I would swear that I do know
The blue bliss of her eye :
" Tarry, maid, maid," I bid her ;
   But she hastened by.
Do you know where she has hid her,
   Maid July ?

Yet in truth it needs must be
   The flight of her is old ;
Yet in truth it needs must be,
   For her nest, the earth, is cold.

No more in the poolèd Even
    Wade her rosy feet,
Dawn-flakes no more plash from them
    To poppies 'mid the wheat.

She has muddied the day's oozes
    With her petulant feet ;
Scared the clouds that floated
    As sea-birds they were,
Slow on the cœrule
    Lulls of the air,
Lulled on the luminous
    Levels of air :
She has chidden in a pet
    All her stars from her ;
Now they wander loose and sigh
    Through the turbid blue,
Now they wander, weep, and cry—
    Yea, and I too—
" Where are you, sweet July,
    Where are you ? "

Who hath beheld her footprints,
    Or the pathway she goes ?
Tell me, wind, tell me, wheat,
    Which of you knows ?
Sleeps she swathed in the flushed Arctic
    Night of the rose ?
Or lie her limbs like Alp-glow
    On the lily's snows ?

Gales, that are all-visitant,
   Find the runaway ;
And for him who findeth her
   (I do charge you say)
I will throw largesse of broom
   Of this summer's mintage,
I will broach a honey-bag
   Of the bee's best vintage.
Breezes, wheat, flowers sweet,
   None of them knows !
How then shall we lure her back
   From the way she goes ?
For it were a shameful thing,
   Saw we not this comer
Ere Autumn camp upon the fields
   Red with rout of Summer.

When the bird quits the cage,
   We set the cage outside,
With seed and with water,
   And the door wide,
Haply we may win it so
   Back to abide.
Hang her cage of earth out
   O'er Heaven's sunward wall,
Its four gates open, winds in watch
   By reinèd cars at all ;
Relume in hanging hedgerows
   The rain-quenched blossom,
And roses sob their tears out
   On the gale's warm heaving bosom ;

Shake the lilies till their scent
   Over-drip their rims,
That our runaway may see
   We do know her whims :
Sleek the tumbled waters out
   For her travelled limbs ;
Strew and smooth blue night thereon,
   There will—O not doubt her !—
The lovely sleepy lady lie,
   With all her stars about her !
               Francis Thompson.

31. SEPTEMBER

SPRING is past and over these many days,
   Spring and summer.   The leaves of September
      droop,
Yellowing and all but dead on the patient trees.
Nor is there any hope in me.   I walk
Slowly homeward.   Night is as empty and dark
Behind my eyes as it is dark without
And empty round about me and over me.
But, looking up, suddenly I see
Leaves in the upthrown light of a street lamp shine
Clear and luminous, young and so transparent,
They seem but the coloured foam of air, green fire,
No more than the scarce embodied thoughts of leaves ;
And it is spring within that circle of light.
Oh, magical brightness !—the old leaves are made new.
In the mind, too, some coloured accident
Of beauty revives and makes all young again.
A chance light meaningless shines and it is Spring.
               Aldous Huxley.

32. TEMPER IN OCTOBER

HE rode at furious speed to Broken Edge,
   And he was very angry, very small ;
But God was kind, knowing he needed not
A scolding, nor a swift unpleasant fall,
Nor any high reproach of soul at all.
" It matters not," said Reason and Good Sense ;
" Absurd to let a trifle grow immense."
" It matters very much," said Busy Brain ;
" You cannot be content and calm again,
For you are angry in a righteous cause."
" Poor, queer old Waxy ! " laughed the hips and haws.
" God has a sense of humour," said a ball
Of orange-gold inside a spindle-berry—
" And ' Christ our Lorde is full exceeding merrie.' "

He lingered in the lane at Broken Edge,
Bryony berries burned from every hedge ;
Snails in the deep wet grass of fairy rings
Told him of unimaginable things.
Love was in all the colours of the sky,
Love in the folded shadows of the high
Blue hills, as quiet as any Easter Eve.
(O fool, O blind and earthbound thus to grieve !)

He turned his horse.   Through level sunset-gleams
He saw a sudden little road that curled
And climbed elusive to a sky of dreams.
His anger over Broken Edge was hurled
To scatter into nothing on a gust
Of wind which brought the twilight to the trees.

The drifted leaves, the white October dust
Hiding the beechnuts for the squirrels' store,
Heard the low whisper spoken on his knees :—
" God, You have made a very perfect world,
Don't let me spoil it ever any more."

V. L. Edminson.

33. TO IRON FOUNDERS AND OTHERS

WHEN you destroy a blade of grass
 You poison England at her roots :
Remember no man's foot can pass
Where evermore no green life shoots.

You force the birds to wing too high
Where your unnatural vapours creep :
Surely the living rocks shall die
When birds no rightful distance keep.

You have brought down the firmament
And yet no heaven is more near ;
You shape huge deeds without event,
And half-made men believe and fear.

Your worship is your furnaces,
Which, like old idols, lost obscenes,
Have molten bowels ; your vision is
Machines for making more machines.

O, you are busied in the night,
Preparing destinies of rust ;
Iron misused must turn to blight
And dwindle to a tetter'd crust.

The grass, forerunner of life, has gone,
But plants that spring in ruins and shards
Attend until your dream is done :
I have seen hemlock in your yards.

The generations of the worm
Know not your loads piled on their soil ;
Their knotted ganglions shall wax firm
Till your strong flagstones heave and toil.

When the old hollow'd earth is crack'd,
And when, to grasp more power and feasts,
Its ores are emptied, wasted, lack'd,
The middens of your burning beasts

Shall be raked over till they yield
Last priceless slags for fashionings high,
Ploughs to wake grass in every field,
Chisels men's hands to magnify.

Gordon Bottomley.

34. DUCKS
I

FROM troubles of the world
   I turn to ducks,
Beautiful comical things
Sleeping or curled
Their heads beneath white wings
By water cool,
Or finding curious things
To eat in various mucks
Beneath the pool,

Tails uppermost, or waddling
Sailor-like on the shores
Of ponds, or paddling
—Left ! right !—with fanlike feet
Which are for steady oars
When they (white galleys) float
Each bird a boat
Rippling at will the sweet
Wide waterway . . .
When night is fallen *you* creep
Upstairs, but drakes and dillies
Nest with pale water-stars,
Moonbeams and shadow bars,
And water-lilies :
Fearful too much to sleep
Since they've no locks
To click against the teeth
Of weasel and fox.
And warm beneath
Are eggs of cloudy green
Whence hungry rats and lean
Would stealthily suck
New life, but for the mien,
The bold ferocious mien
Of the mother-duck.

II

Yes, ducks are valiant things
On nests of twigs and straws,
And ducks are soothy things
And lovely on the lake

When that the sunlight draws
Thereon their pictures dim
In colours cool.
And when beneath the pool
They dabble, and when they swim
And make their rippling rings,
O ducks are beautiful things!

But ducks are comical things :—
As comical as you.
Quack!
They waddle round, they do.
They eat all sorts of things,
And then they quack.
By barn and stable and stack
They wander at their will,
But if you go too near
They look at you through black
Small topaz-tinted eyes
And wish you ill.
Triangular and clear
They leave their curious track
In mud at the water's edge,
And there amid the sedge
And slime they gobble and peer
Saying " Quack! quack!"

III

When God had finished the stars and whirl of coloured
    suns
He turned His mind from big things to fashion little
    ones,

Beautiful tiny things (like daisies) He made, and then
He made the comical ones in case the minds of men
      Should stiffen and become
      Dull, humourless and glum :
And so forgetful of their Maker be
As to take even themselves—*quite seriously.*
Caterpillars and cats are lively and excellent puns :
All God's jokes are good—even the practical ones !
And as for the duck, I think God must have smiled
    a bit
Seeing those bright eyes blink on the day He fashioned
    it.
And He's probably laughing still at the sound that
    came out of its bill !

                    F. W. Harvey.

35. EVERYONE SANG

EVERYONE suddenly burst out singing ;
    And I was filled with such delight
As prisoned birds must find in freedom
Winging wildly across the white
Orchards and dark green fields ; on ; on ; and out of
    sight.

Everyone's voice was suddenly lifted,
And beauty came like the setting sun.
My heart was shaken with tears, and horror
Drifted away. . . . O, but every one
Was a bird ; and the song was wordless ; the singing
    will never be done.

              Siegfried Sassoon.

36. THE WAGGONER

THE old waggon drudges through the miry lane
    By the skulking pond where the pollards frown,
Notched, dumb, surly images of pain ;
    On a dulled earth the night droops down.

Wincing to slow and wistful airs
    The leaves on the shrubbed oaks know their hour,
And the unknown wandering spoiler bares
    The thorned black hedge of a mournful shower.

Small bodies fluster in the dead brown wrack
    As the stumbling shaft-horse jingles past,
And the waggoner flicks his whip a crack :
    The odd light flares on shadows vast

Over the lodges and oasts and byres
    Of the darkened farm ; the moment hangs wan
As though nature flagged and all desires.
    But in the dim court the ghost is gone

From the hug-secret yew to the penthouse wall,
    And stooping there seems to listen to
The waggoner leading the gray to stall,
    As centuries past itself would do.

                        Edmund Blunden.

37. MOONLIT APPLES

AT the top of the house the apples are laid in rows,
    And the skylight lets the moonlight in, and those
Apples are deep-sea apples of green.   There goes
    A cloud on the moon in the autumn night.

A mouse in the wainscot scratches, and scratches, and
 then
There is no sound at the top of the house of men
Or mice ; and the cloud is blown, and the moon again
 Dapples the apples with deep-sea light.

They are lying in rows there, under the gloomy beams ;
On the sagging floor ; they gather the silver streams
Out of the moon, those moonlit apples of dreams,
 And quiet is the steep stair under.

In the corridors under there is nothing but sleep.
And stiller than ever on orchard boughs they keep
Tryst with the moon, and deep is the silence, deep
 On moon-washed apples of wonder.

      John Drinkwater.

38. MEMORY

IN silence and in darkness memory wakes
 Her million sheathèd buds and breaks
That day-long winter when the light and noise
And hard bleak breath of the outward-looking will
Made barren her tender soil, when every voice
Of her million airy birds was muffled or still.

One bud-sheath breaks :
One sudden voice awakes.
What change grew in our hearts seeing one night
That moth-winged ship drifting across the bay,
Her broad sail dimly white
On cloudy waters and hills as vague as they ?

Some new thing touched our spirit with distant
    delight,
Half-seen, half-noticed, as we loitered down,
Talking in whispers, to the little town,
    Down from the narrow hill
    Talking in whispers, for the air so still
Imposed its stillness on our lips and made
A quiet equal with the equal shade
That filled the slanting walk. That phantom now
Slides with slack canvas and unwhispering prow
Through the dark sea that this dark room has made.
Or the night of the closed eyes will turn to-day
And all day's colours start out of the gray.
The sun burns on the water. The tall hills
Push up their shady groves into the sky
And fail and cease where the intense light spills
Its parching torrent on the gaunt and dry
Rock of the further mountains, whence the snow
That softened their harsh edges long is gone.
    And nothing tempers now
The hot flood falling on the barren stone.

    O memory, take and keep
All that my eyes, your servants, bring you home—
Those other days beneath the low white dome
    Of smooth-spread clouds that creep
    As slow and soft as sleep,
When shade grows pale and the cypress stands upright,
    Distinct in the cool light,
Rigid and solid as a dark, hewn stone;
    And many another night

That melts in darkness on the narrow quays
And changes every colour and every tone
And soothes the waters to a softer ease,
When under constellations coldly bright
The homeward sailors sing their way to bed
On ships that motionless in harbour float.
The circling harbour lights flash green and red ;
And, out beyond, a steady travelling boat
Breaking the swell with slow industrious oars
    At each stroke pours
Pale lighted water from the lifted blade.
Now in the painted houses all around
    Slow darkening windows call
The empty unwatched middle of the night.
The tide's few inches rise without a sound.
On the black promontory's windless head,
The last awake, the fireflies rise and fall
And tangle up their dithering skeins of light.

    O memory, take and keep
All that my eyes, your servants, bring you home !
    Thick through the changing year
The unexpected, rich-charged moments come,
    That you 'twixt wake and sleep
In the lids of the closed eyes shall make appear.
    This is life's certain good,
Though in the end it be not good at all
    When the dark end arises
And the stripped, startled spirit must let fall
    The amulets that could
Prevail with life's but not death's sad devices.

Then, like a child from whom an older child
Forces its gathered treasures,
Its beads and shells and strings of withered flowers,
   Tokens of recent pleasures,
The soul must lose in eyes weeping and wild
   Those prints of vanished hours.

Edward Shanks.

39. EVENING OVER THE FOREST

WATCH.
   What is it you see ?

The stark bough of an oak.
Beyond it the evening sky.
Clear, clear the evening sky
And green like a green pearl.

Did you hear ?
What did you hear ?

The harsh cry of a bird,
Beyond it the evening sky.
Still, still the evening sky
And green like a green pearl.

Oh, search.
What is it you see ?

Fiery snowy little cloud
Sailing to sleep in the sky.

Dim, dim the evening sky
Like a deep green pearl.

Come away.
Come away.

Beatrice Mayor.

40. THE LATE, LAST ROOK

THE old gilt vane and spire receive
   The last beam eastward striking ;
The first shy bat to peep at eve
Has found her to his liking.
The western heaven is dull and grey,
The last red glow has followed day.

The late, last rook is housed and will
With cronies lie till morrow ;
If there's a rook loquacious still
In dream he hunts a furrow,
And flaps behind a spectre team,
Or ghostly scarecrows walk his dream.

Ralph Hodgson.

41. THE SUNKEN GARDEN

SPEAK not—whisper not ;
   Here bloweth thyme and bergamot ;
Softly on the evening hour
Secret herbs their spices shower,

Dark-spiked rosemary and myrrh,
Lean-stalked, purple lavender ;
Hides within her bosom, too,
All her sorrows, bitter rue.

Breathe not—trespass not ;
Of this green and darkling spot,
Latticed from the moon's beams,
Perchance a distant dreamer dreams ;
Perchance upon its darkening air,
The unseen ghosts of children fare,
Faintly swinging, sway and sweep,
Like lovely sea-flowers in its deep ;
While, unmoved, to watch and ward,
'Mid its gloomed and daisied sward,
Stands with bowed and dewy head
That one little leaden lad.

Walter de la Mare.

42. MY GARDEN

A GARDEN is a lovesome thing, God wot !
    Rose plot,
  Fringed pool,
Ferned grot—
    The veriest school
    Of peace ; and yet the fool
Contends that God is not—
Not God ! in gardens ! when the eve is cool ?
    Nay, but I have a sign ;
     'Tis very sure God walks in mine.

T. E. Brown.

43. THE DESERTED GARDEN
Ypres, July 1917

I LOVE this garden, for you used to play
    About its haunted shadows long ago :
The years glide by in waves of blossom gay,
    And tides of jewelled snow.

Each summer brings the drowsy bees that **doze**
    Among the lazy flowers till you return :
Around your arbour the clematis grows,
    And red carnations burn.

Your spirit ever haunts my memory,
    As some faint echo when the hour is late :
The tall white hollyhocks wait dreamily
    Beside the crooked gate.

The jessamine that twinkles in the light,
    Still watches idly through the window-pane :
While scented stocks do weave their spell each night,
    In case you come again.

The silent trees remember, for they cast
    Their form just where your footsteps seem to lag :
The honeysuckle spreads its trailers fast,
    And the old palings sag.

Nor do the pensive columbines forget,
    Because they still unfold their little flowers :
The fragrance of devotion lingers yet
    Across the listless hours.

There is no stir ; the eager moments fly,
    Breathless as embers dwindling in the gloom :
No leaf dare fall ; the shadows loiter by,
    Like gnomes about my room.

Above the lattice where the roses cling,
    The fire-flies dart as they did long ago :
My heart would break if any bird should sing,
    Or if the wind should blow.
                Alasdair Alpin MacGregor.

44. A DESERTED HOME

HERE where the fields lie lonely and untended,
    Once stood the old house grey among the trees,
Once to the hills rolled the waves of the cornland—
    Long waves and golden, softer than the sea's.

Long, long ago has the ploughshare rusted,
    Long has the barn stood roofless and forlorn ;
But oh ! far away are some who still remember
    The songs of the young girls binding up the corn.

Here where the windows shone across the darkness,
    Here where the stars once watched above the fold,
Still watch the stars, but the sheepfold is empty ;
    Falls now the rain where the hearth glowed of old.

Here where the leagues of melancholy lough-sedge
    Moan in the wind round the grey forsaken shore,
Once waved the corn in the mid-month of autumn,
    Once sped the dance when the corn was on the floor.
                Sidney Royse Lysaght.

45. THE BARN

RAIN-SUNKEN roof, grown green and thin
    For sparrows' nests and starlings' nests ;
Dishevelled eaves ; unwieldy doors,
Cracked rusty pump, and oaken floors,
And idly-pencilled names and jests
   Upon the posts within.

The light pales at the spider's lust,
The wind tangs through the shattered pane :
An empty hop-poke spreads across
The gaping frame to mend the loss
And keeps out sun as well as rain,
   Mildewed with clammy dust.

The smell of apples stored in hay
And homely cattle-cake is there.
Use and disuse have come to terms,
The walls are hollowed out by worms,
But men's feet keep the mid-floor bare
   And free from worse decay.

All merry noise of hens astir
Or sparrows squabbling on the roof
Comes to the barn's broad open door ;
You hear upon the stable floor
Old hungry Dapple strike his hoof,
   And the blue fan-tail's whir.

The barn is old, and very old,
But not a place of spectral fear.
Cobwebs and dust and speckling sun
Come to old buildings every one.
Long since they made their dwelling here,
   And here you may behold

Nothing but simple wane and change ;
Your tread will wake no ghost, your voice
Will fall on silence undeterred.
No phantom wailing will be heard,
Only the farm's blithe cheerful noise ;
   The barn is old, not strange.

Edmund Blunden.

46. ROADS

I LOVE roads :
   The goddesses that dwell
Far along them invisible
Are my favourite gods.

Roads go on
While we forget, and are
Forgotten like a star
That shoots and is gone.

On this earth 'tis sure
We men have not made
Anything that doth fade
So soon, so long endure :

The hill road wet with rain
In the sun would not gleam
Like a winding stream
If we trod it not again.

They are lonely
While we sleep, lonelier
For lack of the traveller
Who is now a dream only.

From dawn's twilight
And all the clouds like sheep
On the mountains of sleep
They wind into the night.

The next turn may reveal
Heaven : upon the crest
The close pine clump, at rest
And black, may Hell conceal.

Often footsore, never
Yet of the road I weary,
Though long and steep and dreary,
As it winds on for ever.

Helen of the roads,
The mountain ways of Wales
And the Mabinogion tales
Is one of the true gods,

Abiding in the trees,
The threes and fours so wise,
The larger companies,
That by the roadside be,

And beneath the rafter
Else uninhabited
Excepting by the dead ;
And it is her laughter

At morn and night I hear
When the thrush cock sings
Bright irrelevant things,
And when the chanticleer

Calls back to their own night
Troops that make loneliness
With their light footsteps' press,
As Helen's own are light.

Now all roads lead to France
And heavy is the tread
Of the living ; but the dead
Returning lightly dance :

Whatever the road bring
To me or take from me,
They keep me company
With their pattering,

Crowding the solitude
Of the loops over the downs,
Hushing the roar of towns
And their brief multitude.

Edward Thomas

47. THE HOMECOMING OF THE SHEEP

THE sheep are coming home in Greece.
    Hark the bells on every hill !
Flock by flock, and fleece by fleece,
Wandering wide a little piece
Thro' the evening red and still,
Stopping where the pathways cease,
Cropping with a hurried will.

Thro' the cotton-bushes low
Merry boys with shouldered crooks
Close them in a single row,
Shout among them as they go
With one bell-ring o'er the brooks.
Such delight you never know
Reading it from gilded books.

Before the early stars are bright
Cormorants and sea-gulls call,
And the moon comes large and white
Filling with a lovely light
The ferny curtained waterfall.
Then sleep wraps every bell up tight
And the climbing moon grows small.

Francis Ledwidge.

48. OUT IN THE DARK

O UT in the dark over the snow
   The fallow fawns invisible go
With the fallow doe ;
And the winds blow
Fast as the stars are slow.

Stealthily the dark haunts round
And, when the lamp goes, without sound
At a swifter bound
Than the swiftest hound,
Arrives, and all else is drowned ;

And star and I and wind and deer
Are in the dark together—near,
Yet far,—and fear
Drums in my ear
In that sage company drear.

How weak and little is the light,
All the universe of sight,
Love and delight,
Before the might,
If you love it not, of night.

Edward Thomas.

49. DRIVING SHEEP

T HE green east flows with the tides of the rose
   Between the bars of night, half-drawn.
The moon shines cold and faint on the fold
   Where sheep glimmer, gray in the dawn.

Oh, thin like a dream their sad cries seem,
  Caught high above time and space ;
And old as the world, from out fleece dew-pearled,
  Gazes each meek sheep-face.
Dazed with sleep, and numb, the sheep-women come
  And open the field gate wide.
The sheep surge out in an idiot rout,
  Like gray foam swept on a tide.
Keep steady, move slow, we've three miles to go
  To Grantchester from Chalk Field pen.
Herd them up all the way, lest some go astray,
  Of our imbecile two score and ten.
Unreasoning, blind, each poor unhinged mind
  Takes its thought from the sheep next ahead.
Through each hedge gate (if you reach it too late)
  They charge, wild and pale, like the dead.
Their lilting bleat, their sharp, scuttling feet,
  Are strange, strange as dreams before day,
And . . . counting the sheep . . . we sway . . . into
    sleep . . .
  And trail along . . . foolish as they.

The wide tides of gold surge, quiet and cold ;
  The green west turns deep blue ;
The moon's worn slip very soon will dip,
  Like a pale night-bird, from view.
There seems no sound in the world all round
  But of horn feet and quavering cries
In the young, cold hour . . . Like flame, like a flower,
  The sun springs, huge with surprise.

                                        Rose Macaulay.

50. THE DOWNS

O BOLD majestic downs, smooth, fair and lonely ;
   O still solitude, only matched in the skies ;
  Perilous in steep places,
  Soft in the level races,
Where sweeping in phantom silence the cloudland flies;
With lovely undulation of fall and rise ;
  Entrenched with thickets thorned,
By delicate miniature dainty flowers adorned !

I climb your crown, and lo ! a sight surprising
Of sea in front uprising, steep and wide :
  And scattered ships ascending
  To heaven, lost in the blending
Of distant blues, where water and sky divide,
Urging their engines against wind and tide,
  And all so small and slow
They seem to be wearily pointing the way they would
    go.

The accumulated murmur of soft plashing,
Of waves on rocks dashing and searching the sands,
  Takes my ear, in the veering
  Baffled wind, as rearing
Upright at the cliff, to the gullies and rifts he stands ;
And his conquering surges scour out over the lands ;
  While again at the foot of the downs
He masses his strength to recover the topmost crowns.
                Robert Bridges.

51. THE DOWNS

OH ! the downs high to the cool sky ;
    And the feel of the sun-warmed moss ;
And each cardoon, like a full moon,
Fairy-spun of the thistle floss ;
And the beech grove, and a wood dove,
And the trail where the shepherds pass ;
And the lark's song, and the wind song,
And the scent of the parching grass !

John Galsworthy.

52. SHEPHERD APOLLO

CLIMB with me, Laomedon's white fleeces,
    Upward to the hilltops, up to Ida,
To unshaded dews and earliest dawning.
Young and lustrous, god and yet a servant,
As a star past rock and tree I climb.
Raise your heads erect, ye flocks, and listen
To the note I strike from off my lyre !
They have heard, they stand each head erected ;
Thus they wait the Grazing-Tune that woos
Slowly to the ridges and the sky.
I have struck it : all submissive listen,
Till they feed in mystery, advancing,
Drawn to solemn paces by a spell ;
Then to sharper strains one way they hurry,
Fleece by fleece around me, till I strike
Sweet, soft notes that lay them down to slumber,
I beside them, where the sun no more
Falls across us, but the chilling moonlight :

There we sleep, my flock and I together,
I, a god, though servant of a king.

Michael Field.

63. SONG OF POPLARS

SHEPHERD, to yon tall poplars tune your flute :
    Let them pierce keenly, subtly shrill,
The slow blue rumour of the hill ;
Let the grass cry with an anguish of evening gold,
And the great sky be mute.

Then hearken how the poplar trees unfold
Their buds, yet close and gummed and blind,
In airy leafage of the mind,
Rustling in silvery whispers the twin-hued scales
That fade not nor grow old.

" Poplars and fountains and you cypress spires
Springing in dark and rusty flame,
Seek you aught that hath a name ?
Or say, say : Are you all an upward agony
Of undefined desires ?

" Say, are you happy in the golden march
Of sunlight all across the day ?
Or do you watch the uncertain way
That leads the withering moon on cloudy stairs
Over the heaven's wide arch ?

" Is it towards sorrow or towards joy you lift
The sharpness of your trembling spears ?
Or do you seek, through the grey tears
That blur the sky, in the heart of the triumphing blue,
A deeper, calmer rift ? "

So ; I have tuned my music to the trees,
And there were voices, dim below
Their shrillness, voices swelling slow
In the blue murmur of hills, and a golden cry
And then vast silences.

Aldous Huxley.

54. OAK AND OLIVE

I

THOUGH I was born a Londoner,
    And bred in Gloucestershire,
I walked in Hellas years ago
    With friends in white attire :
And I remember how my soul
    Drank wine as pure as fire.

And when I stand by Charing Cross
    I can forget to hear
The crash of all those smoking wheels,
    When those cold flutes and clear
Pipe with such fury down the street,
    My hands grow moist with fear.

And there's a hall in Bloomsbury
    No more I dare to tread,
For all the stone men shout at me
    And swear they are not dead ;
And once I touched a broken girl
    And knew that marble bled.

II

But when I walk in Athens town
    That swims in dust and sun,
Perverse, I think of London then,
    Where massive work is done,
And with what sweep at Westminster
    The rayless waters run.

I ponder how from Attic seed
    There grew an English tree,
How Byron like his heroes fell,
    Fighting a country free,
And Swinburne took from Shelley's lips
    The kiss of Poetry.

And while our poets chanted Pan
    Back to his pipes and power,
Great Verrall, bending at his desk,
    And searching hour on hour
Found out old gardens, where the wise
    May pluck a Spartan flower.

III

When I go down the Gloucester lanes
    My friends are deaf and blind :
Fast as they turn their foolish eyes
    The Maenads leap behind,
And when I hear the fire-winged feet,
    They only hear the wind.

Have I not chased the fluting Pan
    Through Cranham's sober trees ?
Have I not sat on Painswick Hill
    With a nymph upon my knees,
And she as rosy as the dawn,
    And naked as the breeze ?

IV

But when I lie in Grecian fields,
    Smothered in asphodel,
Or climb the blue and barren hills,
    Or sing in woods that smell
With such hot spices of the South
    As mariners might sell—

Then my heart turns where no sun burns,
    To lands of glittering rain,
To fields beneath low-clouded skies
    New-widowed of their grain,
And Autumn leaves like blood and gold
    That strew a Gloucester lane.

V

Oh, well I know sweet Hellas now,
    And well I knew it then,
When I with starry lads walked out—
    But ah, for home again !
Was I not bred in Gloucestershire,
    One of the Englishmen !

                          J. E. Flecker.

55. NEW YEAR'S EVE, 1913

OH, Cartmel bells ring soft to-night,
   And Cartmel bells ring clear,
But I lie far away to-night,
   Listening with my dear ;

Listening in a frosty land
   Where all the bells are still
And the small-windowed bell-towers stand
   Dark under heath and hill.

I thought that, with each dying year,
   As long as life should last,
The bells of Cartmel I should hear
   Ring out an aged past :

The plunging, mingling sounds increase
   Darkness's depth and height,
The hollow valley gains more peace
   And ancientness to-night :

The loveliness, the fruitfulness,
   The power of life lived there
Return, revive, more closely press
   Upon that midnight air.

But many deaths have place in men
   Before they come to die ;
Joys must be used and spent, and then
   Abandoned and passed by.

Earth is not ours ; no cherished space
    Can hold us from life's flow,
That bears us thither and thence by ways
    We knew not we should go.

Oh, Cartmel bells ring loud, ring clear,
    Through midnight deep and hoar,
A year new-born, and I shall hear
    The Cartmel bells no more.

                                Gordon Bottomley.

56. BY AVON STREAM

THE jonquils bloom round Samarcand.—
    Maybe ; but lulled by Avon stream,
By hawthorn-scented breezes fanned,
    'Twere mere perversity to dream
        Of Samarcand.

A very heaven the Javan isle !—
    Fond fancy, whither wilt thou stray ?
While bluest skies benignant smile
    On Avon meads, why prate to-day
        Of Javan isle ?

The bulbul 'plains by Omar's shrine.—
    But still I hold, and ever must,
Lark's *tirra-lirra* more divine ;
    And Stratford Church guards dearer dust
        Than Omar's shrine.

                                Arthur Henry Bullen.

57. MARLBOROUGH

I

CROUCHED where the open upland billows down
  Into the valley where the river flows,
She is as any other country town,
  That little lives or marks or hears or knows.

And she can teach but little. She has not
  The wonder and the surging and the roar
Of striving cities. Only things forgot
  That once were beautiful, but now no more,

Has she to give us. Yet to one or two
  She first brought knowledge, and it was for her
To open first our eyes, until we knew
  How great, immeasurably great, we were.

I, who have walked along her downs in dreams,
  And known her tenderness and felt her might,
And sometimes by her meadows and her streams
  Have drunk deep-storied secrets of delight,

Have had my moments there, when I have been
  Unwittingly aware of something more,
Some beautiful aspect that I had seen
  With mute unspeculative eyes before ;

Have had my times, when, though the earth did wear
  Her self-same trees and grasses, I could see
The revelation that is always there,
  But somehow is not always clear to me.

II

So, long ago, one halted on his way
   And sent his company and cattle on :
His caravans trooped darkling far away
   Into the night, and he was left alone.

And he was left alone.   And, lo, a man
   There wrestled with him till the break of day,
The brook was silent and the night was wan.
   And when the dawn was come, he passed away.

The sinew of the hollow of his thigh
   Was shrunken, as he wrestled there alone.
The brook was silent but the dawn was nigh.
   The stranger named him Israel and was gone.

And the sun rose on Jacob ; and he knew
   That he was no more Jacob, but had grown
A more immortal vaster spirit, who
   Had seen God face to face, and still lived on.

The plain that seemed to stretch away to God,
   The brook that saw and heard and knew no fear,
Were now the self-same soul as he who stood
   And waited for his brother to draw near.

For God had wrestled with him, and was gone.
   He looked around, and only God remained.
The dawn, the desert, he and God were one.
   —And Esau came to meet him, travel-stained.

III

So, there, when sunset made the downs look new
   And earth gave up her colours to the sky,
And far away the little city grew
   Half into sight, new-visioned was my eye.

I, who have lived, and trod her lovely earth,
   Raced with her winds and listened to her birds,
Have cared but little for their worldly worth,
   Nor sought to put my passion into words.

But now it's different; and I have no rest
   Because my hand must search, dissect and spell
The beauty that is better not expressed,
   The thing that all can feel, but none can tell.
             Charles Hamilton Sorley.

58. THE BALLIOL ROOKS, 1885

THE winter is dead, and the spring is a-dying,
   And summer is marching o'er mountain and
      plain,
And tossing and tumbling and calling and crying
   The Balliol rooks are above us again;
And watching them wheel on unwearied wings,
I question them softly of vanished things.

   Caw, caw, says every rook,
   To the dreamer his dream, to the scholar his book.
   Caw, caw, but the things for me
   Are the windy sky and the windy tree!

O rooks, have you leant from your heights and
    harkened
  From year to year to the whirl below ?
While the suns have flamed and the days have
    darkened,
  Have you marked men ceaselessly come and go,
Loiter a little while here and pass
As the ripple on water, the shadow on grass ?

Caw, caw, says every rook,
To the dreamer his dream, to the scholar his book.
Caw, caw, but the things for me
Are the windy sky and the windy tree !

The monk with his orisons heavenward rolling,
  The friar of black, and the friar of grey ;
The schoolman stern, and the cavalier trolling
  In court and in cloister his roundelay,
The singer sweet and the preacher pale—
O rooks, can you tell me their wondrous tale ?

Caw, caw, says every rook,
To the dreamer his dream, to the scholar his book
Caw, caw, but the things for me
Are the windy sky and the windy tree !

And we that are heirs to their paths and places,
  To the alleys dim and the sunlit towers,
With our hearts on fire, and our eager faces,
  Still hasting along with the hasting hours ;

O rooks, I pray you, come, tell me true :
Was it better the old ? is it better the new ?

Caw, caw, says every rook,
To the dreamer his dream, to the scholar his book.
Caw, caw, but the things for me
Are the windy sky and the windy tree !

And they that shall follow upon us hereafter,
  The men unknown of the unborn years ;
Will they move you at all with their grief and laughter,
  Will you reck, O rooks, of their hopes and fears ;
Or will you but circle scornfully,
And mock at them as you mock at me ?

Caw, caw, says every rook,
To the dreamer his dream, to the scholar his book.
Caw, caw, but the things for me
Are the windy sky and the windy tree !
                              Frederick S. Boas.

59. AT GRAFTON

God laughed when He made Grafton
    That's under Bredon Hill,
A jewel in a jewelled plain.
The seasons work their will
On golden thatch and crumbling stone,
And every soft-lipped breeze
Makes music for the Grafton men
In comfortable trees.

God's beauty over Grafton
Stole into roof and wall,
And hallowed every pavèd path
And every lowly stall,
And to a woven wonder
Conspired with one accord
The labour of the servant,
The labour of the Lord.

And momently to Grafton
Comes in from vale and wold
The sound of sheep unshepherded,
The sound of sheep in fold,
And, blown along the bases
Of lands that set their wide
Frank brows to God, comes chanting
The breath of Bristol tide.

John Drinkwater.

60. OLTON POOLS

Now June walks on the waters,
    And the cuckoo's last enchantment
Passes from Olton pools.

Now dawn comes to my window
Breathing midsummer roses,
And scythes are wet with dew.

Is it not strange for ever
That, bowered in this wonder,
Man keeps a jealous heart ? . . .

That June and the June waters
And birds and dawn-lit roses,
Are gospels in the wind,

Fading upon the deserts,
Poor pilgrim revelations ? . . .
Hist . . . over Olton pools !

John Drinkwater.

61. THE ALDE

How near I walked to Love,
    How long, I cannot tell.
I was like the Alde that flows
Quietly through green level lands,
So quietly, it knows
Their shape, their greenness and their shadows well ;
And then undreamingly for miles it goes
And silently, beside the sea.

Seamews circle over,
The winter wildfowl wings,
Long and green the grasses wave
Between the river and the sea.
The sea's cry, wild or grave,
From bank to low bank of the river rings ;
But the uncertain river, though it crave
The sea, knows not the sea.

Was that indeed salt wind ?
Came that noise from falling
Wild waters on a stony shore ?
Oh, what is this new troubling tide
Of eager waves that pour
Around and over, leaping, parting, recalling ? . . .
How near I moved (as day to same day wore)
And silently, beside the sea !

John Freeman.

62. THE LITTLE WAVES OF BREFFNY

THE grand road from the mountain goes shining to
the sea,
And there is traffic on it and many a horse and cart,
But the little roads of Cloonagh are dearer far to me,
And the little roads of Cloonagh go rambling through
my heart.

A great storm from the ocean goes shouting o'er the
hill,
And there is glory in it and terror on the wind,
But the haunted air of twilight is very strange and still,
And the little winds of twilight are dearer to my
mind.

The great waves of the Atlantic sweep storming on
their way,
Shining green and silver with the hidden herring
shoal,

But the Little Waves of Breffny have drenched my
heart in spray,
And the Little Waves of Breffny go stumbling
through my soul.

Eva Gore-Booth.

63. CARROWMORE

IT's a lonely road through bogland to the lake at
Carrowmore,
And a sleeper there lies dreaming where the water laps
the shore ;
Though the moth-wings of the twilight in their purples
are unfurled,
Yet his sleep is filled with music by the masters of the
world.

There's a hand is white as silver that is fondling with
his hair :
There are glimmering feet of sunshine that are dancing
by him there :
And half-open lips of faery that were dyed a faery red
In their revels where the Hazel Tree its holy clusters
shed.

" Come away," the red lips whisper, " all the world is
weary now ;
'Tis the twilight of the ages and it's time to quit the
plough.
Oh, the very sunlight's weary ere it lightens up the
dew,
And its gold is changed and faded before it falls to you.

" Though your colleen's heart be tender, a tenderer
heart is near.

What's the starlight in her glances when the stars are
shining clear ?

Who would kiss the fading shadow when the flower-
face glows above ?

'Tis the beauty of all Beauty that is calling for your
love."

Oh, the great gates of the mountain have opened once
again,

And the sound of song and dancing falls upon the ears
of men,

And the Land of Youth lies gleaming, flushed with
rainbow light and mirth,

And the old enchantment lingers in the honey-heart
of earth.

A. E.

64. CORRYMEELA

OVER here in England I'm helpin' wi' the hay,
   An' I wisht I was in Ireland the livelong day ;
Weary on the English hay, an' sorra take the wheat !
   Och ! Corrymeela an' the blue sky over it.

There' a deep dumb river flowin' by beyont the heavy
trees,

   This livin' air is moithered wi' the bummin' o' the
   bees ;

I wisht I'd hear the Claddagh burn go runnin' through
the heat

   Past Corrymeela, wi' the blue sky over it.

The people that's in England is richer nor the Jews,
   There' not the smallest young gossoon but thravels
     in his shoes !
I'd give the pipe between me teeth to see a barefut
   child,
   Och ! Corrymeela an' the low south wind.

Here's hands so full o' money an' hearts so full o' care,
   By the luck o' love ! I'd still go light for all I did
     go bare.
" God save ye, *colleen dhas*," I said : the girl she
   thought me wild.
   Far Corrymeela, an' the low south wind.

D'ye mind me now, the song at night is mortial hard
   to raise,
   The girls are heavy goin' here, the boys are ill to
     plase ;
When one'st I'm out this workin' hive, 'tis I'll be back
   again—
   Ay, Corrymeela, in the same soft rain.

The puff o' smoke from one ould roof before an'
   English town !
   For a *shaugh* wid Andy Feelan here I'd give a silver
     crown,
For a curl o' hair like Mollie's ye'll ask the like in vain,
   Sweet Corrymeela, an' the same soft rain.
                 Moira O'Neill.

65. MERRION SQUARE

GREY clouds on the tinted sky,
  A drifting moon, a quiet breeze
Drooping mournfully to cry
In the branches of the trees.

The crying wind, the sighing trees,
The ruffled stars, the darkness falling
Down the sky, and on the breeze
A belated linnet calling.

James Stephens.

66. SONG OF THE LARKS AT DAWN

SHEPHERDS who pastures seek
  At dawn may see
From Falterona's peak
  Above Camaldoli
Gleam, beyond forests and wildernesses bleak,
  Both shores of Italy.
Fallen apart are the terrible clouds of the morning
  And men lift up their eyes.

Heaven's troubled continents
  Are rifted, torn :
Thunders, in their forest tents,
  Still seethe and sullenly mourn
When aloft, from the gulfs and the sheer ascents,
  Is a music born.
Hark to that music, laggard mists of the morning,
  And men, lift up your eyes !

For scarce can eye see light
  When the ear's aware
That virginals exquisite
  Are raining from the air—
With sun and pale moon mingling their delight—
  Adorations everywhere !
Now listen and yield the vanquish'd stars of the
    morning
  And men lift up their eyes.

Eddy of golden dust—
  Halo of rays—
Thrilling up, up, as they must
  Die of the life they praise—
The larks, the larks ! that to the earth entrust
  Only their sleeping-place.
From rugged wolds and rock-bound valleys of morning
  The larks like mist arise.

Earth sends them up from hills,
  Her wishes small,
Her cloud of griefs, her wills
  To burst from her own thrall,
And to burn away what chains the soul or chills
  In the God and fount of all.
Open your gates, O ye cities faint for morning,
  And men, lift up your eyes !

Open ! Night's blue Pantheon,
  Thy dark roof-ring
For that escaping pæan
  Of tremblers on the wing

At the unknown threshold of the empyrean
    In myriads soft to sing.
Give way before them, temple-veils of the morning,
    And men, lift up your eyes !

They ascend, ere the red beam
    On heaven grows strong,
Into that amazing stream
    Of Dawn—and float along
In the future, for the future is their dream
    Who roof the world with song.
Open your flowers, O ye mountains spread for morning
    And men, lift up your eyes !

Hark ! it grows less and less—
    But nothing mars
That rapture beyond guess—
    Beyond our senses' bars—
They drink the virgin Light, the measureless,
    And in it fade, like stars.
They have gone past, the dew-like spirits of morning
    Beyond the uplifted eyes.

Between two lamps suspended,
    Of Life and Death,
Sun-marshalled and moon-tended
    Man's swift soul journeyeth
To be borne out of the life it hath transcended
    Still, still on a breath ! . . .
To-day we too are the wingèd sons of the morning,
    To-day we will arise !

                                        Herbert Trench.

67. THE DARKLING THRUSH

I LEANT upon a coppice gate
    When Frost was spectre-gray,
And Winter's dregs made desolate
    The weakening eye of day.
The tangled bine-stems scored the sky
    Like strings from broken lyres,
And all mankind that haunted nigh
    Had sought their household fires.

The land's sharp features seemed to be
    The Century's corpse outleant,
His crypt the cloudy canopy,
    The wind his death-lament.
The ancient pulse of germ and birth
    Was shrunken hard and dry,
And every spirit upon earth
    Seemed fervourless as I.

At once a voice burst forth among
    The bleak twigs overhead
In a full-hearted evensong
    Of joy illimited ;
An aged thrush, frail, gaunt, and small,
    In blast-beruffled plume,
Had chosen thus to fling his soul
    Upon the growing gloom.

So little cause for carollings
    Of such ecstatic sound
Was written on terrestrial things
    Afar or nigh around,

That I could think there trembled through
   His happy good-night air
Some blessed Hope, whereof he knew
   And I was unaware.

           Thomas Hardy.

68. BLACKBIRD

HE comes on chosen evenings,
   My blackbird bountiful, and sings
Over the gardens of the town
Just at the hour the sun goes down.
His flight across the chimneys thick,
By some divine arithmetic,
Comes to his customary stack,
And couches there his plumage black,
And there he lifts his yellow bill,
Kindled against the sunset, till
These suburbs are like Dymock woods
Where music has her solitudes,
And while he mocks the winter's wrong
Rapt on his pinnacle of song,
Figured above our garden plots
Those are celestial chimney-pots.

           John Drinkwater.

69. THE BELLS OF HEAVEN

'TWOULD ring the bells of Heaven
   The wildest peal for years,
If Parson lost his senses
And people came to theirs,

And he and they together
Knelt down with angry prayers
For tamed and shabby tigers,
And dancing dogs and bears,
And wretched, blind pit-ponies,
And little hunted hares.

Ralph Hodgson.

70. THE SNARE

I HEAR a sudden cry of pain !
  There is a rabbit in a snare :
Now I hear the cry again,
  But I cannot tell from where.

But I cannot tell from where
  He is calling out for aid ;
Crying on the frightened air,
  Making everything afraid.

Making everything afraid,
  Wrinkling up his little face,
As he cries again for aid ;
  And I cannot find the place !

And I cannot find the place
  Where his paw is in the snare :
Little one ! Oh, little one !
  I am searching everywhere.

James Stephens.

71. THE DONKEY

WHEN fishes flew and forests walked
    And figs grew upon thorn,
Some moment when the moon was blood
    Then surely I was born ;

With monstrous head and sickening cry
    And ears like errant wings,
The devil's walking parody
    On all four-footed things.

The tattered outlaw of the earth,
    Of ancient crooked will ;
Starve, scourge, deride me : I am dumb,
    I keep my secret still.

Fools !   For I also had my hour ;
    One far fierce hour and sweet :
There was a shout about my ears,
    And palms before my feet.

                    Gilbert Keith Chesterton.

72. MILK FOR THE CAT

WHEN the tea is brought at five o'clock,
    And all the neat curtains are drawn with care,
The little black cat with bright green eyes
Is suddenly purring there.

At first she pretends, having nothing to do,
She has come in merely to blink by the grate,
But, though tea may be late or the milk may be sour,
She is never late.

And presently her agate eyes
Take a soft large milky haze,
And her independent casual glance
Becomes a stiff hard gaze.

Then she stamps her claws or lifts her ears,
Or twists her tail and begins to stir,
Till suddenly all her lithe body becomes
One breathing trembling purr.

The children eat and wriggle and laugh';
The two old ladies stroke their silk :
But the cat is grown small and thin with desire,
Transformed to a creeping lust for milk.

The white saucer like some full moon descends
At last from the clouds of the table above ;
She sighs and dreams and thrills and glows,
Transfigured with love.

She nestles over the shining rim,
Buries her chin in the creamy sea ;
Her tail hangs loose ; each drowsy paw
Is doubled under each bending knee.

A long dim ecstasy holds her life ;
Her world is an infinite shapeless white,
Till her tongue has curled the last holy drop,
Then she sinks back into the night,

Draws and dips her body to heap
Her sleepy nerves in the great arm-chair,
Lies defeated and buried deep
Three or four hours unconscious there.

Harold Monro.

73. TO A BLACK GREYHOUND

SHINING black in the shining light,
   Inky black in the golden sun,
Graceful as the swallow's flight,
   Light as swallow, wingèd one,
Swift as driven hurricane—
   Double-sinewed stretch and spring,
Muffled thud of flying feet,
   See the black dog galloping,
   Hear his wild foot-beat.

See him lie when the day is dead,
   Black curves curled on the boarded floor
Sleepy eyes, my sleepy-head—
   Eyes that were aflame before.
Gentle now, they burn no more ;
   Gentle now and softly warm,
With the fire that made them bright
   Hidden—as when after storm
   Softly falls the night.

God of speed, who makes the fire —
   God of Peace, who lulls the same—
God who gives the fierce desire,
   Lust for blood as fierce as flame—

God who stands in Pity's name—
   Many may ye be or less,
Ye who rule the earth and sun :
   Gods of strength and gentleness,
     Ye are ever one.

                  Julian Grenfell.

74. TIM, AN IRISH TERRIER

IT'S wonderful dogs they're breeding now :
   Small as a flea or large as a cow ;
But my old lad Tim he'll never be bet
By any dog that ever he met.
" Come on," says he, " for I'm not kilt yet."

No matter the size of the dog he'll meet,
Tim trails his coat the length o' the street.
D'ye mind his scars an' his ragged ear,
The like of a Dublin Fusilier ?
He's a massacree dog that knows no fear.

But he'd stick to me till his latest breath ;
An' he'd go with me to the gates of death.
He'd wait for a thousand years, maybe,
Scratching the door an' whining for me
If myself were inside in Purgatory.

So I laugh when I hear thim make it plain
That dogs and men never meet again.
For all their talk who'd listen to thim,
With the soul in the shining eyes of him ?
Would God be wasting a dog like Tim ?

                  W. M. Letts.

75. THE TURKISH TRENCH DOG

NIGHT held me as I crawled and scrambled near
        The Turkish lines.   Above, the mocking stars
Silvered the curving parapet, and clear
Cloud-latticed beams o'erflecked the land with bars ;
I, crouching, lay between
Tense-listening armies, peering through the night,
Twin giants bound by tentacles unseen.
Here in dim-shadowed light
I saw him, as a sudden movement turned
His eyes towards me, glowing eyes that burned
A moment ere his snuffling muzzle found
My trail ; and then as serpents mesmerise
He chained me with those unrelenting eyes,
That muscle-sliding rhythm, knit and bound
In spare-limbed symmetry, those perfect jaws
And soft-approaching pitter-patter paws.
Nearer and nearer like a wolf he crept—
That moment had my swift revolver leapt—
But terror seized me, terror born of shame
Brought flooding revelation.   For he came
As one who offers comradeship deserved,
An open ally of the human race,
And sniffing at my prostrate form unnerved
He licked my face !

Geoffrey Dearmer.

76. SONG FROM CALLIRRHOË

I DANCE and dance !   Another faun,
    A black one, dances on the lawn.
He moves with me, and when I lift
My heels his feet directly shift :

I can't outdance him though I try ;
He dances nimblier than I.
I toss my head, and so does he ;
What tricks he dares to play with me !
I touch the ivy in my hair ;
Ivy he has and finger there.
The spiteful thing to mock me so !
I will outdance him !   Ho, ho, ho !

Michael Field.

77. LULLABY

STRIPPED thee when thou hast and girt
    Thy clean night-shirt,
Leap into the soft snug bed ;
Lay down thy head ;
Sleep, and in thy white cot be
A picture for the stars to see.

Cling not to the game that's dead ;
Be glad instead,
After all thy falls and frowns,
That silence drowns
All that any star might see
To make such clear light sad for thee.

Sleep, sleep ;
Down, down,
Through silence good and deep,
Down, down ;

Sink as through a well, each trace
Or of spite, of sulk or frown,
Dying out from thy still face
Till asleep thou dreaming lie,—
A sight to charm the moon on high
And hold her longer in the sky.

T. Sturge Moore.

78. EX ORE INFANTIUM

LITTLE Jesus, wast Thou shy
    Once, and just so small as I ?
And what did it feel like to be
Out of Heaven, and just like me ?
Didst Thou sometimes think of *there*,
And ask where all the angels were ?
I should think that I would cry
For my house all made of sky ;
I would look about the air,
And wonder where my angels were ;
And at waking 'twould distress me—
Not an angel there to dress me !

Hadst Thou ever any toys,
Like us little girls and boys ?
And didst Thou play in Heaven with all
The angels, that were not too tall,
With stars for marbles ?   Did the things
Play *Can you see me ?* through their wings ?

Didst Thou kneel at night to pray,
And didst Thou join Thy hands, this way ?
And did they tire sometimes, being young,
And make the prayer seem very long ?
And dost Thou like it best, that we
Should join our hands to pray to Thee ?
I used to think, before I knew,
The prayer not said unless we do.
And did Thy Mother at the night
Kiss Thee, and fold the clothes in right ?
And didst Thou feel quite good in bed,
Kissed, and sweet, and Thy prayers said ?

Thou canst not have forgotten all
That it feels like to be small :
And Thou know'st I cannot pray
To Thee in my father's way—
When Thou wast so little, say,
Couldst Thou talk Thy Father's way ?—
So, a little Child, come down
And hear a child's tongue like Thy own ;
Take me by the hand and walk,
And listen to my baby-talk.
To Thy Father show my prayer
(He will look, Thou art so fair),
And say : " O Father, I, Thy Son,
Bring the prayer of a little one."

And He will smile, that children's tongue
Has not changed since Thou wast young !
Francis Thompson.

79. SHAKESPEARE

IF many a daring spirit must discover
   The chartless world, why should they glory lack
Because athwart the skyline they sank over ?
Few, few, the shipmen be that have come back.

Yet one, wrecked oft, hath by a giddy cord
The rugged head of Destiny regain'd—
One from the maelstrom's lap hath swum aboard—
One from the polar sleep himself unchain'd.

And he, acquainted well with every tone
Of madness whining in his shroudage slender,
From storm and mutiny emerged alone
Self-righted from the dreadful self-surrender :

Rich from the isles where sojourn long is death,
Won back to cool Thames and Elizabeth,
Sea-weary, yes, but human still, and whole,—
A circumnavigator of the soul.

Herbert Trench.

80. I LIKE TO THINK OF SHAKESPEARE

I LIKE to think of Shakespeare, not as when
   In our old London of the spacious time
He took all amorous hearts with honeyed rhyme ;
Or flung his jest at Burbage and at Ben ;
Or speared the flying follies with his pen ;
Or, in deep hour, made Juliet's love sublime ;
Or from Lear's kindness and Iago's crime
Caught tragic hint of heaven's dark way with men.

These were great memories, but he laid them down.
And when, with brow composed and friendly tread,
He sought the little streets of Stratford town,
That knew his dreams and soon must hold him dead,
I like to think how Shakespeare pruned his rose,
And ate his pippin in his orchard close.

E. K. Chambers.

81. FRIENDS BEYOND

WILLIAM DEWY, Tranter Reuben, Farmer Ledlow late at plough,
    Robert's kin, and John's and Ned's,
And the Squire, and Lady Susan, lie in Mellstock
churchyard now !

" Gone," I call them, gone for good, that group of
local hearts and heads ;
    Yet at mothy curfew-tide,
And at midnight when the noon-heat breathes it back
from walls and leads,

They've a way of whispering to me—fellow-wight
who yet abide—
    In the muted, measured note
Of a ripple under archways, or a lone cave's
stillicide :

" We have triumphed : this achievement turns the
bane to antidote,
    Unsuccesses to success,
Many thought-worn eves and morrows to a morrow
free of thought.

" No more need we corn and clothing, feel of old ter-
      restrial stress ;
            Chill detraction stirs no sigh ;
Fear of death has even bygone us : death gave all
      that we possess."

W. D. : " Ye mid burn the old bass-viol that I set
            such value by."
Squire :   " You may hold the manse in fee,
            You may wed my spouse, may let my children's
            memory of me die."

Lady : " You may have my rich brocades, my laces ;
            take each household key ;
            Ransack coffer, desk, bureau ;
            Quiz the few poor treasures hid there, con the
            letters kept by me."

Far. : " Ye mid zell my favourite heifer, ye mid let
            the charlock grow,
            Foul the grinterns, give up thrift."
Wife : " If ye break my best blue china, children, I
            shan't care or ho."

All :   " We've no wish to hear the tidings how the
            people's fortunes shift ;
            What your daily doings are ;
            Who are wedded, born, divided ; if your lives
            beat slow or swift.

" Curious not the least are we if our intents you
    make or mar,
        If you quire to our old tune,
If the City stage still passes, if the weirs still roar
    afar."

Thus, with very gods' composure, freed those crosses
    late and soon
        Which, in life, the Trine allow
(Why, none witteth), and ignoring all that haps
    beneath the moon,

William Dewy, Tranter Reuben, Farmer Ledlow late
    at plough,
        Robert's kin, and John's and Ned's,
And the Squire, and Lady Susan, murmur mildly
    to me now.

                      Thomas Hardy.

82. THE FIDDLER OF DOONEY

WHEN I play on my fiddle in Dooney,
    Folk dance like a wave of the sea ;
My cousin is priest in Kilvarnet,
My brother in Moharabuiee.

I passed my brother and cousin :
They read in their books of prayer ;
I read in my book of songs
I bought at the Sligo fair.

When we come at the end of time,
To Peter sitting in state,
He will smile on the three old spirits,
But call me first through the gate ;

For the good are always the merry,
Save by an evil chance,
And the merry love the fiddle,
And the merry love to dance :

And when the folk there spy me,
They will all come up to me,
With " Here is the fiddler of Dooney ! "
And dance like a wave of the sea.

William Butler Yeats.

83. THE PLOUGHER

SUNSET and silence ; a man ; around him earth
savage, earth broken :
Beside him two horses, a plough !

Earth savage, earth broken, the brutes, the dawn-man
    there in the sunset !
And the plough that is twin to the sword, that is
    founder of cities !

" Brute-tamer, plough-maker, earth-breaker, canst
    hear ?   There are ages between us !
Is it praying you are as you stand there, alone in the
    sunset ?

" Surely our sky-born gods can be nought to you,
  Earth-child and Earth-master !
Surely your thoughts are of Pan, or of Wotan or
  Dana !

" Yet why give thought to the gods ? Has Pan led
  your brutes where they stumble ?
Has Wotan put hands to your plough or Dana
  numbed pain of the childbed ?

" What matter your foolish reply, O man, standing
  lone and bowed earthward.
Your task is a day near its close. Give thanks to
  the night-giving God."

Slowly the darkness falls, the broken lands blend with
  the savage,
The brute-tamer stands by the brutes, by a head's
  breadth only above them !

A head's breadth, ay, but therein is Hell's depth and
  the height up to Heaven,
And the thrones of the gods, and their halls and their
  chariots, purples and splendours.

Padraic Colum.

84. THE PENNY WHISTLE

THE new moon hangs like an ivory bugle
    In the naked frosty blue ;
And the ghylls of the forest, already blackened
    By Winter, are blackened anew.

The brooks that cut up and increase the forest,
    As if they had never known
The sun, are roaring with black hollow voices
    Betwixt rage and a moan.

But still the caravan-hut by the hollies
    Like a kingfisher gleams between :
Round the mossed old hearths of the **charcoal-burners**
    First primroses ask to be seen.

The charcoal-burners are black, but their linen
    Blows white on the line ;
And white the letter the girl is reading
    Under that crescent fine :

And her brother who hides apart in a thicket,
    Slowly and surely playing
On a whistle an old nursery melody,
    Says far more than I am saying.

                                    Edward Thomas.

85. THE MARKET

A MAN came to me at the fair
        And said, " If you've a poet's tongue,
Tumble up and chant the air
That the stars of morning sung.

" I'll pay you, if you sing it nice,
A penny piece."—I answered flat,
" Sixpence is the proper price
For a ballad such as that."

But he stared and wagged his head,
Growling as he passed along,
" Sixpence ! well, I'll see you dead
Before I pay that for a song."

I saw him buy three pints of stout
With the sixpence—dirty lout !

James Stephens.

86. SEUMAS BEG

A MAN was sitting underneath a tree
Outside a village, and he asked me what
Name was upon this place, and said that he
Was never here before. He told a lot
Of stories to me too. His nose was flat.
I asked him how it happened, and he said
The first mate of the *Mary Anne* done that
With a marling spike one day, but he was dead,
And jolly good job too ; and he'd have gone
A long way to have killed him, and he had
A gold ring in one ear ; the other one
" Was bit off by a crocodile, bedad."
That's what he said. He taught me how to chew
He was a real nice man. He liked me too.

James Stephens.

87. TAM I' THE KIRK

O JEAN, my Jean, when the bell ca's the congrega·
tion
Owre valley an' hill wi' the ding frae its iron mou',
When a'body's thochts is set on his ain salvation,
Mine's set on you.

There's a reid rose lies on the Buik o' the Word **afore**
 ye
That was growin' braw on its bush at the keek o' day,
But the lad that pu'd yon flower i' the mornin's glory,
        He canna pray.

He canna pray ; but there's nane i' the kirk will heed
 him
Whaur he sits sae still his lane at the side o' the wa',
For nane but the reid rose kens what my lassie gie'd
 him—
        It an' us twa !

He canna sing for the sang that his ain he'rt raises,
He canna see for the mist that's afore his een,
And a voice drouns the hale o' the psalms an' the
 paraphrases,
        Cryin' " Jean, Jean, Jean ! "

                                        Violet Jacob.

88. THE GOWK

I see the Gowk an' the Gowk sees me
Beside a berry-bush by the apple-tree.
Old Scots Rhyme.

TIB, my auntie's a deil to wark,
    Has me risin' afore the sun ;
Aince her heid is abune her sark
    Then the clash o' her tongue's begun !
Warslin', steerin' wi' hens an' swine,
Naucht kens she o' a freend o' mine—
But the Gowk that bides i' the woods o' Dun
    He kens him fine !

Past the yaird an' ahint the stye,
  O the aipples grow bonnilie !
Tib, my auntie, she canna' spy
  Wha comes creepin' to kep wi' me.
Aye ! she'd sort him, for, dod, she's fell !
Whisht now, Jimmie, an' hide yersel'
An' the wise-like bird i' the aipple-tree
        He winna' tell !

Aprile-month, or the aipples flower,
  Tib, my auntie, will rage an' ca' ;
Jimmie lad, she may rin an' glower—
  What care I ? We'll be far awa' !
Let her seek me the leelang day,
Wha's to tell her the road we'll gae ?
For the cannie Gowk, tho' he kens it a',
        He winna' say !

                 Violet Jacob.

89. THE TWO LAMPLIGHTERS

I NEVER thowt when I grew owd
  I'd tak to leetin' lamps ;
I sud have said, I'd rayther pad
  My hoof on t' road wi' tramps.
But sin I gate that skelp [1] i' t' mine,
  I'm wankle [2] i' my heead ;
So gaffer said, I'd give ower wark
  An' leet town lamps atsteead.

----

[1] Blow.   [2] Unsteady.

At first, when I were liggin' snug
  I' bed, warm as a bee,
'T were hard to rise and get agate
  As sooin as t' clock strake three.
An' I were flaid to hear my steps
  Echoin' on ivery wall ;
An' flaider yet when down by t' church
  Ullets would skreek and call.

But now I'm flaid o' nowt ; I love
  All unkerd [1] sounds o' t' neet,
Frae childer talkin' i' their dreams
  To t' tramp o' p'licemen' feet.
But most of all I love to hark
  To t' song o' t' birds at dawn ;
They wakken up afore it gloams,
  When t' dew ligs thick on t' lawn.

If I feel lonesome, up I look
  To t' sky aboon my heead ;
An' theer's yon stars all glestrin' breet,
  Like daisies in a meead.
But sometimes, when I'm glowerin' up,
  I see the Lord hissen ;
He's doutin' all yon lamps o' Heaven
  That shines on mortal men.

He lowps alang frae star to star,
  As cobby [2] as can be ;
Mebbe He reckons fowk's asleep,
  Wi' niver an eye to see.

[1] Strange, eerie.   [2] Active.

But I hae catched Him at his wark,
   For all He maks no din ;
He leaves a track o' powder'd gowd [1]
   To show where He has bin.

He's got big lamps an' laatle lamps,
   An' lamps that twinkles red ;
I'm capped to see Him dout 'em all
   Afore I'm back i' bed.
But He don't laik about His wark,
   Or stop to hark to t' birds ;
He minds His business, does the Lord,
   An' wastes no gaumless words.

I grow more like Him ivery day,
   For all I walk so lame ;
An', happen, there will coom a time
   I'll beat Him at His game.
Thrang as Throp's wife, I'll dout my lamps
   Afore He's gotten so far ;
An' then I'll shout—" I've won my race,
   I've bet Him by a star."

F. W. Moorman.

90. A BALLAD-MAKER

ONCE I loved a maiden fair,
   Over the hills and far away,
Lands she had and lovers to spare,
Over the hills and far away.

[1] The Milky Way.

And I was stooped and troubled sore,
And my face was pale, and the coat I wore
Was thin as my supper the night before.
　　Over the hills and far away.

Once I passed in the autumn late,
　　Over the hills and far away,
Her bawn and byre and painted gate,
　　Over the hills and far away.
She was leaning there in the twilight space,
Sweet sorrow was on her fair young face,
And her wistful eyes were away from the place—
　　Over the hills and far away.

Maybe she thought as she watched me come,
　　Over the hills and far away,
With my awkward stride, and my face so glum,
　　Over the hills and far away,
" Spite of his stoop, he still is young ;
They say he goes the Shee among,
Ballads he makes, I've heard them sung
　　Over the hills and far away."

She gave me good night in gentle wise,
　　Over the hills and far away,
Shyly lifting to mine, dark eyes,
　　Over the hills and far away.
What could I do but stop and speak,
And she no longer proud but meek ?
She plucked me a rose like her wild-rose cheek—
Over the hills and far away.

To-morrow, Mavourneen a sleeveen weds,
Over the hills and far away,
With corn in haggard and cattle in sheds,
Over the hills and far away.
And I who have lost her—the dear, the rare—
Well, I got me this ballad to sing at the fair,
'Twill bring enough money to drown my care,
Over the hills and far away.

Padraic Colum.

91. THE PENALTY OF LOVE

IF love should count you worthy, and should deign
    One day to seek your door and be your guest,
  Pause ! ere you draw the bolt and bid him rest,
If in your old content you would remain,
For not alone he enters ; in his train
    Are angels of the mist, the lonely quest,
    Dreams of the unfulfilled and unpossessed,
And sorrow, and Life's immemorial pain.

He wakes desires you never may forget,
    He shows you stars you never saw before,
    He makes you share with him, for evermore,
The burden of the world's divine regret.
How wise you were to open not ! and yet,
    How poor if you should turn him from the door !

Sidney Royse Lysaght.

92. I WENT INTO THE FIELDS

I WENT into the fields, but you were there
    Waiting for me, so all the summer flowers
Were only glimpses of your starry powers ;
Beautiful and inspired dust they were.

I went down by the waters, and a bird
Sang with your voice in all the unknown tones
Of all that self of you I have not heard,
So that my being felt you to the bones.

I went into the house, and shut the door
To be alone, but you were there with me ;
All beauty in a little room may be,
Though the roof lean, and muddy be the floor.

Then in my bed I bound my tired eyes
To make a darkness for my weary brain ;
But like a presence you were there again,
Being and real, beautiful and wise,

So that I could not sleep, and cried aloud,
" You strange grave thing, what is it **you**
    would say ? "
The redness of your dear lips dimmed to grey,
The waters ebbed, the moon hid in a cloud.

              John Masefield.

93. RENOUNCEMENT

I MUST not think of thee; and, tired yet strong,
  I shun the love that lurks in all delight—
 The love of thee—and in the blue heaven's height,
And in the dearest passage of a song.
Oh, just beyond the sweetest thoughts that throng
 This breast, the thought of thee waits hidden yet
    bright;
 But it must never, never come in sight;
I must stop short of thee the whole day long.
But when sleep comes to close each difficult day,
 When night gives pause to the long watch I keep,
And all my bonds I needs must loose apart,
Must doff my will as raiment laid away,—
 With the first dream that comes with the first sleep,
I run, I run, I am gathered to thy heart.

Alice Meynell.

94. DAWN SHALL OVER LETHE BREAK

LADY, when your lovely head
  Sinks to lie among the Dead,
And the quiet Places keep
You that so divinely sleep:
Then the Dead shall blessèd be
With a New Solemnity.
For such beauty so descending
Pledges them that death is ending.
Sleep your fill :—But when you wake
Dawn shall over Lethe break.

Hilaire Belloc.

95. LELANT

(In Memory of Thomasine Trenoweth, aged 23)

THE little meadow by the sand,
    Where Tamsin lies, is ringed about
With acres of the scented thyme.
The salt wind blows in all that land ;
The great clouds pace across the skies ;
Rare wanderers from the ferry climb.
One might sleep well enough, no doubt,
    Where Tamsin lies.

Tamsin has sunshine now and wind,
And all in life she might not have,
The silence and the utter peace
That tempest-winnowed spirits find
On slopes that front the western wave.
The white gulls circle without cease
    O'er Tamsin's grave.

             E. K. Chambers.

. 96. THE GREAT LOVER

I HAVE been so great a lover : filled my days
    So proudly with the splendour of Love's praise,
The pain, the calm, and the astonishment,
Desire illimitable, and still content,
And all dear names men use, to cheat despair,
For the perplexed and viewless streams that bear
Our hearts at random down the dark of life.
Now, ere the unthinking silence on that strife

Steals down, I would cheat drowsy Death so far,
My night shall be remembered for a star
That outshone all the suns of all men's days.
Shall I not crown them with immortal praise
Whom I have loved, who have given me, dared with me
High secrets, and in darkness knelt to see
The inenarrable godhead of delight ?
Love is a flame ;—we have beaconed the world's night.
A city :—and we have built it, these and I.
An emperor :—we have taught the world to die.
So, for their sakes I loved, ere I go hence,
And the high cause of Love's magnificence,
And to keep loyalties young, I'll write those names
Golden for ever, eagles, crying flames,
And set them as a banner, that men may know,
To dare the generations, burn, and blow
Out on the wind of Time, shining and streaming . . .

These I have loved :
            White plates and cups, clean-gleaming,
Ringed with blue lines ; and feathery, faery dust ;
Wet roofs, beneath the lamp-light ; the strong crust
Of friendly bread ; and many-tasting food ;
Rainbows ; and the blue bitter smoke of wood ;
And radiant raindrops couching in cool flowers ;
And flowers themselves, that sway through sunny
      hours,
Dreaming of moths that drink them under the moon ;
Then, the cool kindliness of sheets, that soon
Smooth away trouble ; and the rough male kiss
Of blankets ; grainy wood ; live hair that is

Shining and free ; blue-massing clouds ; the keen
Unpassioned beauty of a great machine ;
The benison of hot water ; furs to touch ;
The good smell of old clothes ; and other such—
The comfortable smell of friendly fingers,
Hair's fragrance, and the musty reek that lingers
About dead leaves and last year's ferns . . .

        Dear names,
And thousand other throng to me ! Royal flames ;
Sweet water's dimpling laugh from tap or spring ;
Holes in the ground ; and voices that do sing ;
Voices in laughter, too ; and body's pain,
Soon turned to peace ; and the deep-panting train ;
Firm sands ; the little dulling edge of foam
That browns and dwindles as the wave goes home ;
And washen stones, gay for an hour ; the cold
Graveness of iron ; moist black earthen mould ;
Sleep ; and high places ; footprints in the dew ;
And oaks ; and brown horse-chestnuts, glossy-new ;
And new-peeled sticks ; and shining pools on grass ;—
All these have been my loves. And these shall
   pass,
Whatever passes not, in the great hour,
Nor all my passion, all my prayers, have power
To hold them with me through the gate of Death.
They'll play deserter, turn with the traitor breath,
Break the high bond we made, and sell Love's trust
And sacramented covenant to the dust.
—Oh, never a doubt but, somewhere, I shall wake,
And give what's left of love again, and make
New friends, now strangers . . .

But the best I've known,
Stays here, and changes, breaks, grows old, is blown
About the winds of the world, and fades from brains
Of living men, and dies.

Nothing remains.

O dear my loves, O faithless, once again
This one last gift I give : that after men
Shall know, and later lovers, far-removed,
Praise you, " All these were lovely " ; say, " He
    loved."

Rupert Brooke,

97. CLIFTON

I'M here at Clifton, grinding at the mill
   My feet for thrice nine barren years have trod ;
But there are rocks and waves at Scarlett still,
   And gorse runs riot in Glen Chass—thank God !

Alert, I seek exactitude of rule,
   I step, and square my shoulders with the squad ;
But there are blaeberries on old Barrule,
   And Langness has its heather still—thank God !

There is no silence here : the truculent quack
   Insists with acrid shriek my ears to prod,
And, if I stop them, fumes ; but there's no lack
   Of silence still on Carraghyn—thank God !

Pragmatic fibs surround my soul, and bate it
   With measured phrase, that asks the assenting nod ;
I rise, and say the bitter thing, and hate it—
   But Wordsworth's castle's still at Peel—thank God !

O broken life !   O wretched bits of being,
   Unrhythmic, patched, the even and the odd !
But Bradda still has lichens worth the seeing,
   And thunder in her caves—thank God ! thank God !
                        T. E. Brown.

98. A CIDER SONG

To J. S. M.

Extract from a Romance which is not yet written and probably
never will be.

THE wine they drink in Paradise
   They make in Haute Lorraine ;
God brought it burning from the sod
To be a sign and signal rod
That they that drink the blood of God
Shall never thirst again.

The wine they praise in Paradise
They make in Ponterey,
The purple wine of Paradise,
But we have better at the price ;
It's wine they praise in Paradise,
It's cider that they pray.

The wine they want in Paradise
They find in Plodder's End,
The apple wine of Hereford,
Of Hafod Hill and Hereford,
Where woods went down to Hereford,
And there I had a friend.

The soft feet of the blessed go
In the soft western vales,
The road the silent saints accord,
The road from Heaven to Hereford,
Where the apple wood of Hereford
Goes all the way to Wales.

Gilbert Keith Chesterton.

99. FORTUNATUS NIMIUM

I HAVE lain in the sun,
 I have toiled as I might,
I have thought as I would,
And now it is night.

My bed full of sleep,
My heart of content,
For friends that I met
The way that I went.

I welcome fatigue,
While frenzy and care
Like thin summer clouds
Go melting in air.

To dream as I may
And awake when I will
With the song of the birds
And the sun on the hill.

Or death—were it death—
To what should I wake
Who loved in my home
All life for its sake ?

What good have I wrought ?
I laugh to have learned
That joy cannot come
Unless it is earned.

For a happier lot
Than God giveth me
It never hath been
Nor ever shall be.

Robert Bridges.

100. SOLITUDE

WHEN you have tidied all things for the night,
    And while your thoughts are fading to their
       sleep,
You'll pause a moment in the late firelight,
Too sorrowful to weep.

The large and gentle furniture has stood
In sympathetic silence all the day
With that old kindness of domestic wood ;
Nevertheless the haunted room will say :
" Some one must be away."

The little dog rolls over half awake,
Stretches his paws, yawns, looking up at you,
Wags his tail very slightly for your sake,
That you may feel he is unhappy too.

A distant engine whistles, or the floor
Creaks, or the wandering night-wind bangs a door.

Silence is scattered like a broken glass.
The minutes prick their ears and run about,
Then one by one subside again and pass
Sedately in, monotonously out.

You bend your head and wipe away a tear.
Solitude walks one heavy step more near.

Harold Monro.

101. HEAVY WITH THOUGHT

HEAVY with thought, and burdened with desire,
  O sturdy pilgrim, is it thus you go ?
And is it thus accoutred, is it so,
They start upon the path who dare aspire
To climb the bastion where the peaks of fire,
Home of the thunder burn against the blue ?
And some have reached the goal—but not as you,
Heavy with thought and burdened with desire.

And I, poor cripple, neither faint nor tire ;
My armour is the plumage of the dove,
My thoughts are feathers and my wings are love ;
Higher I soar, and higher yet, and higher,
The dust, the noise, the darkness far above,
Upborne by thought and wingèd with desire.

Cecil Spring-Rice.

102. THE NIGHT

MOST Holy Night, that still dost keep
  Thy keys of all the doors of sleep,
To me when my tired eyelids close
  Give thou repose.

And let the fair lament of them
That chant the day's dead requiem
　　Make in my ears, who wakeful lie,
　　　　Sweet Lullaby.

Let them that guard the hornèd Moon
By my bedside their memories croon,
　　So shall I have new dreams and blest
　　　　In my brief rest.

Fold thy great wings about my face,
Hide day-dawn from my resting-place,
　　And cheat me into false delight,
　　　　Most Holy Night.

　　　　　　　　　　Hilaire Belloc.

103. LIGHT

THE night has a thousand eyes,
　　And the day but one ;
Yet the light of the bright world dies
　　With the dying sun.

The mind has a thousand eyes,
　　And the heart but one ;
Yet the light of a whole life dies
　　When love is done.

　　　　　　　　　　F. W. Bourdillon.

104. SNUG IN MY EASY CHAIR

SNUG in my easy chair,
  I stirred the fire to flame,
Fantastically fair,
The flickering fancies came,
Born of heart's desire :
Amber woodland streaming ;
Topaz islands dreaming ;
Sunset-cities gleaming,
Spire on burning spire ;
Ruddy-windowed taverns ;
Sunshine-spilling wines ;
Crystal-lighted caverns
Of Golconda's mines ;
Summers, unreturning ;
Passion's crater yearning ;
Troy, the ever-burning ;
Shelley's lustral pyre ;
Dragon-eyes, unsleeping ;
Witches' caldrons leaping ;
Golden galleys sweeping
Out from sea-walled Tyre :
Fancies, fugitive and fair,
Flashed with singing through the air ;
Till, dazzled by the drowsy glare,
I shut my eyes to heat and light ;
And saw, in sudden night,
Crouched in the dripping dark,
With steaming shoulders stark,
The man who hews the coal to feed my fire.
                    Wilfrid Wilson Gibson.

105. MID-MAY, 1918

I

IT shall not me dismay
  That I've grown old and grey ;
Nor tell-tale glass I chide
That will not wrinkles hide :
The visionary gold
That in my heart I hold,
Doth far in worth outshine
All metal from the mine.

II

Of folios I've a store :—
Angelic Henry More,
Lov'd Fuller (wittiest sage)
And Burton's magic page :
There Pliny, Plutarch stand,
Here's Hakewill to my hand,
And thy once far-famed screed,
Apocalyptic Mede.

III

But till the winter eves
Bide there, old printed leaves !
Here's Field o' th' Cloth of Gold
With buttercups untold :
Tall chestnut-candles flare,
Hawthorn makes rich the air,
And tireless cuckoo—hark !—
Calleth from dawn to dark. . . .

       Arthur Henry Bullen.

106. IN MERCER STREET

I

A Piper

A PIPER in the streets to-day
    Set up, and tuned, and started to play,
And away, away, away on the tide
Of his music we started ; on every side
Doors and windows were opened wide,
And men left down their work and came,
And women with petticoats coloured like flame
And little bare feet that were blue with cold,
Went dancing back to the age of gold,
And all the world went gay, went gay,
For half an hour in the street to-day.

II

Rags and Bones

Gather 'em, gather 'em, gather 'em O,
He shouts monotonous, jolting slow
His little truck of rags and bones
Over the uneven cobble stones.
Ever about him clink and crowd
The waifs, a many-coloured cloud
All shrilly clamouring, mad with joy,
For sticky sweet, or painted toy.
Hardly a breath is in the air,
Yet every little windmill there
Goes whirling wildly, as though it knew
With every turn what rapture flew

Through all the heavy street, and stirred
The stagnant air, till the sad bird,
High on the wall, takes heart to sing
And hails the simulated Spring.

III

LARK'S SONG

In Mercer Street the light slants down,
And straightway an enchanted town
Is round him, pinnacle and spire
Flash back, elate, the sudden fire ;
And clear above the silent street
Falls suddenly and strangely sweet
The lark's song.   Bubbling, note on note
Rise fountain-like, o'erflow and float
Tide upon tide, and make more fair
The magic of the sunlit air.
No more the cage can do him wrong,
All is forgotten save his song :
He has forgot the ways of men,
Wide heaven is over him again,
And round him the wide fields of dew
That his first infant mornings knew,
E'er yet the dolorous years had brought
The hours of captive anguish, fraught
With the vile clamour of the street,
The insult of the passing feet,
The torture of the daily round,
The organ's blasphemy of sound.
Sudden some old swift memory brings
The knowledge of forgotten wings,

He springs elate and panting falls
At the rude touch of prison walls.
Silence.   Again the street is grey ;
Shut down the windows.   Work-a-day.

Seumas O'Sullivan.

107. THE SHELL

AND then I pressed the shell
    Close to my ear
And listened well,
And straightway like a bell
Came low and clear
The slow, sad murmur of far distant seas,
Whipped by an icy breeze
Upon a shore
Wind-swept and desolate.
It was a sunless strand that never bore
The footprint of a man,
Nor felt the weight
Since time began
Of any human quality or stir
Save what the dreary winds and waves incur,
And in the hush of waters was the sound
Of pebbles rolling round,
For ever rolling with a hollow sound.
And bubbling sea-weeds as the waters go
Swish to and fro
Their long, cold tentacles of shiny grey.
There was no day,
Nor ever came a night
Setting the stars alight

To wonder at the moon :
Was twilight only and the frightened croon,
Smitten to whimpers, of the dreary wind
And waves that journeyed blind—
And then I loosed my ear—O, it was sweet
To hear a cart go jolting down the street.

James Stephens.

108. ROMANCE

COME, come to me !
    I am the Sea,
I am all that can never be ;
The whirling wave, the steady light
Of ships slow sailing out into the night ;
Wind, wave and leaping spray,
And the lands which are very far away ;
Every rainbow-circled shore,
Where you may stay
A night and a day,
No more !
I kiss your eyes and leave them blind ;
I am around you and above ;
I am the road that lies before,
And behind ;
I am Morning—I am Love !
I shake my gleaming
My sun-splashed wings,
Whilst you lie dreaming
Of other things.
The sun shakes your grating,
The wind's at the door ;

Oh ! ride forth, for all the world is waiting,
And come back no more !

Am I not fair
With my wishing cap on my gold hair ?
Am I not fleet
Who have feathered shoulders and wingèd feet ?
Listen ! listen ! have you heard
Such a song ever,
As now beneath the wandering moon I sing ?
Each wild-winged bird
Whose throat is mad with Spring
Has sought to learn it and might never !
Listen ! whereso'er I pass
Laughter stirs among the grass,
And the withered tree
Breaks into leaf,
And Grief
Smiles through heavy eyes, tear-laden,
And becomes my waiting-maiden,
Serving me !

I am the sheath, I am the sword,
And I am flame : I set alight
Cities that men may make
Songs of that burning for my sake,
And yield their souls up at a word.
It may be I shall turn my head
And with my eyes' flash strike you dead,
What matters it ?
You will have lived as only they
Who do my bidding may.

Of what avail to sit
In comfort, ease, and slow decay,
Watching the grey ash, bit by bit,
Crumble away ?
What care though I destroy,
Who have re-christened Death and called him Joy,
And have taught Laughter
To the sharp-visaged, horny-fingered Fates.—
Oh ! if I lead you dancing through Hell's gates
What matter what comes after ?

Come, come to me !
I am the moon, I am the sea;
I am every ship that sails
Trackless waters, knowing not
Where she steers.
I am the light which never fails ;
I am a golden knot
Binding together the loose years.
I sparkle and run
Like ice in the moonlight, like frost in the sun,
And when you have found me, then life has begun.
Therefore be bold,
Of my hand take hold,
And swing in the track of my garment's fold !
Cling to me, follow me, set your heart free ;
I am all that can never be,
A song, a spell, a key of gold,
Which can unlock the earth and the sea :—
Come, come, oh ! come with me !

Lady Margaret Sackville.

109. THE SCHOONER

JUST mark that schooner westward far at sea—
     'Tis but an hour ago
When she was lying hoggish at the quay,
     And men ran to and fro,
And tugged, and stamped, and shoved, and pushed,
    and swore,
And ever and anon, with crapulous glee,
Grinned homage to viragoes on the shore.

So to the jetty gradual she was hauled :
     Then one the tiller took,
And chewed, and spat upon his hand, and bawled ;
     And one the canvas shook
Forth like a mouldy bat ; and one, with nods
And smiles, lay on the bowsprit-end, and called
And cursed the Harbour-master by his gods.

And, rotten from the gunwale to the keel,
     Rat-riddled, bilge-bestank,
Slime-slobbered, horrible, I saw her reel,
     And drag her oozy flank,
And sprawl among the deft young waves, that laughed,
And leapt, and turned in many a sportive wheel,
As she thumped onward with her lumbering draught.

And now, behold ! a shadow of repose
     Upon a line of gray,
She sleeps, that transverse cuts the evening rose—
     She sleeps, and dreams away,
Soft-blended in a unity of rest
All jars, and strifes obscene, and turbulent throes
'Neath the broad benediction of the West—

Sleeps ; and methinks she changes as she sleeps,
      And dies, and is a spirit pure.
Lo ! on her deck an angel pilot keeps
      His lonely watch secure ;
And at the entrance of Heaven's dockyard waits,
Till from Night's leash the fine-breath'd morning leaps,
And that strong hand within unbars the gates.

                 T. E. Brown.

110. A PASSER-BY

WHITHER, O splendid ship, thy white sails crowding,
    Leaning across the bosom of the urgent West,
That fearest nor sea rising, nor sky clouding,
   Whither away, fair rover, and what thy quest ?
   Ah ! soon, when Winter has all our vales opprest,
When skies are cold and misty, and hail is hurling,
   Wilt thou glide on the blue Pacific, or rest
In a summer haven asleep, thy white sails furling.

I there before thee, in the country that well thou
    knowest,
   Already arrived am inhaling the odorous air :
I watch thee enter unerringly where thou goest,
   And anchor queen of the strange shipping there,
   Thy sails for awnings spread, thy masts bare ;
Nor is aught from the foaming reef to the snow-capped,
    grandest
   Peak, that is over the feathery palms more fair
Than thou, so upright, so stately, and still thou
    standest.

And yet, O splendid ship, unhailed and nameless,
   I know not if, aiming a fancy, I rightly divine
That thou hast a purpose joyful, a courage blameless,
   Thy port assured in a happier land than mine.
    But for all I have given thee, beauty enough is thine,
As thou, aslant with trim tackle and shrouding,
   From the proud nostril curve of a prow's line
In the offing scatterest foam, thy white sails crowding
                    Robert Bridges.

111. THE OLD SHIPS

I HAVE seen old ships sail like swans asleep
   Beyond the village which men still call Tyre,
With leaden age o'ercargoed, dipping deep
For Famagusta and the hidden sun
That rings black Cyprus with a lake of fire ;
And all those ships were certainly so old—
Who knows how oft with squat and noisy gun,
Questing brown slaves or Syrian oranges,
The pirate Genoese
Hell-raked them till they rolled
Blood, water, fruit and corpses up the hold.
But now through friendly seas they softly run,
Painted the mid-sea blue or shore-sea green,
Still patterned with the vine and grapes in gold.

But I have seen,
Pointing her shapely shadows from the dawn
An image tumbled on a rose-swept bay,
A drowsy ship of some yet older day ;

And, wonder's breath indrawn,
Thought I—who knows—who knows—but in that
    same
(Fished up beyond Aeæa, patched up new
—Stern painted brighter blue—)
That talkative, bald-headed seaman came
(Twelve patient comrades sweating at the oar)
From Troy's doom-crimson shore,
And with great lies about his wooden horse
Set the crew laughing, and forgot his course.
It was so old a ship—who knows, who knows ?
—And yet so beautiful, I watched in vain
To see the mast burst open with a rose,
And the whole deck put on its leaves again.

                      J. E. Flecker.

112. CARGOES

QUINQUIREME of Nineveh from distant Ophir
    Rowing home to haven in sunny Palestine,
With a cargo of ivory,
And apes and peacocks,
Sandalwood, cedarwood, and sweet white wine.

Stately Spanish galleon coming from the Isthmus,
Dipping through the Tropics by the palm-green shores,
With a cargo of diamonds,
Emeralds, amethysts,
Topazes, and cinnamon, and gold moidores.

Dirty British coaster with a salt-caked smoke-stack
Butting through the Channel in the mad March days,
With a cargo of Tyne coal,
Road-rails, pig-lead,
Firewood, iron-ware, and cheap tin trays.

John Masefield.

113. MESSMATES

HE gave us all a good-bye cheerily
        At the first dawn of day ;
We dropped him down the side full drearily
        When the light died away.
It's a dead dark watch that he's a-keeping there,
And a long, long night that lags a-creeping there,
Where the Trades and the tides roll over him
        And the great ships go by.

He's there alone with green seas rocking him
        For a thousand miles round ;
He's there alone with dumb things mocking him,
        And we're homeward bound.
It's a long, lone watch that he's a-keeping there,
And a dead cold night that lags a-creeping there,
While the months and the years roll over him
        And the great ships go by.

I wonder if the tramps come near enough
        As they thrash to and fro,
And the battle-ships' bells ring clear enough
        To be heard down below ;

If through all the lone watch that he's a-keeping there,
And the long, cold night that lags a-creeping there,
The voices of the sailor-men shall comfort him
> When the great ships go by.

> > *Henry Newbolt.*

114. SEA FEVER

I MUST go down to the seas again, to the lonely sea
> and the sky,
And all I ask is a tall ship and a star to steer her by ;
And the wheel's kick and the wind's song and the white
> sail's shaking,
And a grey mist on the sea's face, and a grey dawn
> breaking.

I must go down to the seas again, for the call of the
> running tide
Is a wild call and a clear call that may not be denied ;
And all I ask is a windy day with the white clouds
> flying,
And the flung spray and the blown spume, and the
> sea-gulls crying.

I must go down to the seas again, to the vagrant gypsy
> life,
To the gull's way and the whale's way where the wind's
> like a whetted knife ;
And all I ask is a merry yarn from a laughing fellow-
> rover,
And quiet sleep and a sweet dream when the long
> trick's over.

> > *John Masefield.*

115. CHORUS FROM HIPPOLYTUS

COULD I take me to some cavern for mine hiding,
   In the hill-tops where the Sun scarce hath trod ;
Or a cloud make the home of mine abiding,
  As a bird among the bird-droves of God !
    Could I wing me to my rest amid the roar
    Of the deep Adriatic on the shore,
Where the water of Eridanus is clear,
  And Phaëthon's sad sisters by his grave
Weep into the river, and each tear
  Gleams, a drop of amber, in the wave !

To the strand of the Daughters of the Sunset,
  The Apple-tree, the singing and the gold ;
Where the mariner must stay him from his onset,
  And the red wave is tranquil as of old ;
    Yea, beyond that Pillar of the End
    That Atlas guardeth, would I wend ;
Where a voice of living waters never ceaseth
  In God's quiet garden by the sea,
And Earth, the ancient life-giver, increaseth
  Joy among the meadows, like a tree.

Gilbert Murray.

116. THE SONG OF THE UNGIRT RUNNERS

WE swing ungirded hips,
    And lightened are our eyes,
The rain is on our lips,
We do not run for prize.

We know not whom we trust
Nor whitherward we fare,
But we run because we must
    Through the great wide air.

The waters of the seas
Are troubled as by storm.
The tempest strips the trees
And does not leave them warm.
Does the tearing tempest pause ?
Do the tree tops ask it why ?
So we run without a cause
    'Neath the big bare sky.

The rain is on our lips,
We do not run for prize.
But the storm the water whips
And the wave howls to the skies.
The winds arise and strike it
And scatter it like sand,
And we run because we like it
    Through the broad bright land.
                        Charles Hamilton Sorley.

117. THE CAVES OF AUVERGNE

HE carved the red deer and the bull
    Upon the smooth cave rock,
Returned from war with belly full,
    And scarred with many a knock,
He carved the red deer and the bull
    Upon the smooth cave rock.

The stars flew by the cave's wide door,
   The clouds wild trumpets blew,
Trees rose in wild dreams from the floor,
   Flowers with dream faces grew
Up to the sky, and softly hung
   Golden and white and blue.

The woman ground her heap of corn,
   Her heart a guarded fire ;
The wind played in his trembling soul
   Like a hand upon a lyre,
The wind drew faintly on the stone
   Symbols of his desire :

The red deer of the forest dark,
   Whose antlers cut the sky,
That vanishes into the mirk
   And like a dream flits by,
And by an arrow slain at last
   Is but the wind's dark body.

The bull that stands in marshy lakes
   As motionless and still
As a dark rock jutting from a plain
   Without a tree or hill ;
The bull that is the sign of life,
   Its sombre, phallic will.

And from the dead, white eyes of them
   The wind springs up anew,
It blows upon the trembling heart,
   And bull and deer renew
Their flitting life in the dim past
   When that dead Hunter drew.

I sit beside him in the night,
   And, fingering his red stone,
I chase through endless forests dark
   Seeking that thing unknown,
That which is not red deer or bull,
   But which by them was shown :

By those stiff shapes in which he drew
   His soul's exalted cry,
When flying down the forest dark
   He slew and knew not why,
When he was filled with song, and strength
   Flowed to him from the sky.

The wind blows from red deer and bull,
   The clouds wild trumpets blare,
Trees rise in wild dreams from the earth,
   Flowers with dream-faces stare,
O Hunter, your own shadow stands
   Within your forest lair !

                  Walter J. Turner.

118. ECSTASY

I SAW a frieze on whitest marble drawn
   Of boys who sought for shells along the shore,
Their white feet shedding pallor in the sea,
The shallow sea, the spring-time sea of green
That faintly creamed against the cold, smooth pebbles.

The air was thin, their limbs were delicate,
The wind had graven their small eager hands
To feel the forests and the dark nights of Asia
Behind the purple bloom of the horizon,
Where sails would float and slowly melt away.

Their naked, pure, and grave unbroken silence
Filled the soft air as gleaming, limpid water
Fills a spring sky those days when rain is lying
In shattered bright pools on the wind-dried roads,
And their sweet bodies were wind-purified.

One held a shell unto his shell-like ear
And there was music carven in his face,
His eyes half-closed, his lips just breaking open
To catch the lulling, mazy, coralline roar
Of numberless caverns filled with singing seas.

And all of them were hearkening as to singing
Of far-off voices thin and delicate,
Voices too fine for any mortal wind
To blow into the whorls of mortal ears—
And yet those sounds flowed from their grave, sweet
        faces.

And as I looked I heard that delicate music,
And I became as grave, as calm, as still
As those carved boys.   I stood upon that shore.
I felt the cool sea dream around my feet,
My eyes were staring at the far horizon :

And the wind came and purified my limbs,
And the stars came and set within my eyes,
And snowy clouds rested upon my shoulders,
And the blue sky shimmered deep within me,
And I sang like a carven pipe of music.

W. J. Turner.

119. THE WAR SONG OF THE SARACENS

WE are they who come faster than fate: we are
they who ride early or late:
We storm at your ivory gate: Pale Kings of the
Sunset, beware!
Not on silk nor in samet we lie, not in curtained
solemnity die
Among women who chatter and cry, and children who
mumble a prayer.
But we sleep by the ropes of the camp, and we rise
with a shout, and we tramp
With the sun or the moon for a lamp, and the spray
of the wind in our hair.

From the lands, where the elephants are, to the forts
of Merou and Balghar,
Our steel we have brought and our star to shine on
the ruins of Rum.
We have marched from the Indus to Spain, and by God
we will go there again;
We have stood on the shore of the plain where the
Waters of Destiny boom.
A mart of destruction we made at Jalula where men
were afraid,

For death was a difficult trade, and the sword was a
    broker of doom ;

And the Spear was a Desert Physician who cured not
    a few of ambition,
And drave not a few to perdition with medicine bitter
    and strong ;
And the shield was a grief to the fool and as bright
    as a desolate pool,
And as straight as the rock of Stamboul when their
    cavalry thundered along :
For the coward was drowned with the brave when our
    battle sheered up like a wave,
And the dead to the desert we gave, and the glory
    to God in our song.

J. E. Flecker.

120. THE WIFE OF LLEW

And Gwydion said to Math, when it was Spring :
    " Come now and let us make a wife for Llew,"
And so they broke broad boughs yet moist with dew,
And in a shadow made a magic ring :
They took the violet and the meadow-sweet
To form her pretty face, and for her feet
They built a mound of daisies on a wing,
And for her voice they made a linnet sing
In the wide poppy blowing for her mouth.
And over all they chanted twenty hours.
And Llew came singing from the azure south
And bore away his wife of birds and flowers.

Francis Ledwidge.

10—P.T.D. 2

121. THE OXEN

CHRISTMAS Eve, and twelve of the clock.
    " Now they are all on their knees,"
An elder said as we sat in a flock
    By the embers in hearthside ease.

We pictured the meek mild creatures where
    They dwelt in their strawy pen,
Nor did it occur to one of us there
    To doubt they were kneeling then.

So fair a fancy few would weave
    In these years !   Yet, I feel,
If someone said on Christmas Eve,
    " Come ; see the oxen kneel

" In the lonely barton by yonder coomb
    Our childhood used to know,"
I should go with him in the gloom,
    Hoping it might be so.

Thomas Hardy.

122. THE LISTENERS

" Is there anybody there ? " said the Traveller,
    Knocking on the moonlit door ;
And his horse in the silence champed the grasses
    Of the forest's ferny floor :
And a bird flew up out of the turret,
    Above the Traveller's head :
And he smote upon the door again a second time ;
    " Is there anybody there ? " he said.

But no one descended to the Traveller ;
   No head from the leaf-fringed sill
Leaned over and looked into his grey eyes,
   Where he stood perplexed and still.
But only a host of phantom listeners
   That dwelt in the lone house then
Stood listening in the quiet of the moonlight
   To that voice from the world of men :
Stood thronging the faint moonbeams on the dark
    stair,
   That goes down to the empty hall,
Hearkening in an air stirred and shaken
   By the lonely Traveller's call.
And he felt in his heart their strangeness,
   Their stillness answering his cry,
While his horse moved, cropping the dark turf,
   'Neath the starred and leafy sky ;
For he suddenly smote on the door, even
   Louder, and lifted his head :—
" Tell them I came, and no one answered,
   That I kept my word," he said.
Never the least stir made the listeners,
   Though every word he spake
Fell echoing through the shadowiness of the still house
   From the one man left awake :
Ay, they heard his foot upon the stirrup,
   And the sound of iron on stone,
And how the silence surged softly backward,
   When the plunging hoofs were gone.

                    Walter de la Mare.

123. THE CHANGELING

Toll no bell for me, dear Father, dear Mother,
      Waste no sighs ;
There are my sisters, there is my little brother
  Who plays in the place called Paradise,
Your children all, your children for ever ;
      But I, so wild,
Your disgrace, with the queer brown face, was never,
  Never, I know, but half your child !

In the garden at play, all day, last summer,
      Far and away I heard
The sweet " tweet-tweet " of a strange new-comer,
  The dearest, clearest call of a bird.
It lived down there in the deep green hollow,
  My own old home, and the fairies say
The word of a bird is a thing to follow,
  So I was away a night and a day.

One evening, too, by the nursery fire,
  We snuggled close and sat round so still,
When suddenly as the wind blew higher,
  Something scratched on the window-sill.
A pinched brown face peered in—I shivered ;
  No one listened or seemed to see ;
The arms of it waved and the wings of it quivered,
  Whoo—I knew it had come for me ;
  Some are as bad as bad can be !
All night long they danced in the rain,
Round and round in a dripping chain,

Threw their caps at the window-pane,
  Tried to make me scream and shout
  And fling the bedclothes all about :
I meant to stay in bed that night,
And if only you had left a light
  They would never have got me out.

  Sometimes I wouldn't speak, you see,
  Or answer when you spoke to me,
Because in the long, still dusks of Spring
You can hear the whole world whispering ;
  The shy green grasses making love,
  The feathers grow on the dear, grey dove,
  The tiny heart of the redstart beat,
  The patter of the squirrel's feet,
The pebbles pushing in the silver streams,
The rushes talking in their dreams,
  The swish-swish of the bat's black wings,
  The wild-wood bluebell's sweet ting-tings,
    Humming and hammering at your ear,
    Everything there is to hear
In the heart of hidden things,
  But not in the midst of the nursery riot,
  That's why I wanted to be quiet,
    Couldn't do my sums, or sing,
    Or settle down to anything.
  And when, for that, I was sent upstairs
  I *did* kneel down to say my prayers ;
But the King who sits on your high church steeple
Has nothing to do with us fairy people !

'Times I pleased you, dear Father, dear Mother,
  Learned all my lessons and liked to play,
And dearly I loved the little pale brother
  Whom some other bird must have called away.
Why did They bring me here to make me
  Not quite bad and not quite good,
Why, unless They're wicked, do They want, in spite,
    to take me
  Back to their wet, wild wood ?
Now, every night I shall see the windows shining,
  The gold lamp's glow, and the fire's red gleam,
While the best of us are twining twigs and the rest of
    us are whining
  In the hollow by the stream.
Black and chill are Their nights on the wold ;
  And They live so long and They feel no pain :
I shall grow up, but never grow old,
I shall always, always be very cold,
  I shall never come back again !

                                    Charlotte Mew.

124. A FAERY SONG

WHEN through a thousand eyes
      Heaven is gleaming,
Troop there folk wee and wise,
  Laden with dreaming ;
Packs full of finest gold
Culled from the river,
Where sunbeams manifold
Shimmer and shiver ;

Packs full of diamonds they
Gathered at morning,
Down by the meadow-way,
Grasses adorning ;
Packs full of lovesongs more
Sweet than a lover's,
Filched from a troubadour
Feathered pelt covers.
Come away !
Come and play
Life with the faeries,
Lest you grow old and grey
Dwelling where care is.

Down from the hillsides green,
Up from the valleys,
Round her Queen Mab, I ween,
All her host rallies ;
For him who wakes to see
—Gladdest of mortals—
Faeryland verily
Opens her portals ;
Every elf on the ground,
Lo, his pack flinging,
See them dance round and round,
Hark to their singing !
Come away !
Come and play
Life with the faeries,
Lest you grow old and grey
Dwelling where care is.

Work-a-day !   Work-a-day !
Counting your sorrow ;
Night is the hour of play
Ere dawns the morrow.
Here there be gold and stones,
Love in full measure ;
He who sleeps lightly owns
Princeliest treasure.
Gather then while ye may
Dreams full of gladness,
Though with the turn of day
Care come and sadness.

Come away !
Come and play
Life with the faeries,
Lest you grow old and grey
Dwelling where care is.
                    Madeleine Nightingale.

125. PISKIES

(Writ in Devon)

THERE'S piskies up to Dartymoor,
    An' tidden gude yew zay there bain't.
I've felt 'em grawpin' at my heart,
I've heard their voices callin' faint,
I've knawed a man be cruel down—
His soul fair stogged an' heavy-like—
Climb up to brawken Zaddle Tor
An' bare his head vor winds to strike.

An' all the gert black mawky griefs,
An' all the pain an' vog an' grime,
Have blawed away and left en clear
Like vuzz-bush vires in swalin' time.
An' what med do so brave a thing
As thic' white spells to tak an' weave,
But li'l piskies' vitty hands,
Or God Himself as give 'em leave ?
But tidden Him would stop an' spy
From Widdicombe to Cranmer Pule,
To maze the schemin' li'l heart
Of every Jacky-Lantern fule !
For mebbe 'tis a lonesome rod
Or heather blooth, or peaty ling,
Or nobbut just a rainy combe—
The spell that meks 'ee tek an' sing.
An' this I knaw, the li'l tods
Be ever callin' silver faint.
There's piskies up to Dartymoor,
An' tidden gude yew zay there bain't.

T. P. Cameron Wilson.

126. THE STOLEN CHILD

WHERE dips the rocky highland
        Of Sleuth Wood in the lake,
There lies a leafy island
Where flapping herons wake
The drowsy water-rats ;
There we've hid our faery vats,

Full of berries,
And of reddest stolen cherries.
Come away, O human child !
To the waters and the wild
With a faery, hand in hand,
For the world's more full of weeping than you
can understand.

Where the wave of moonlight glosses
The dim gray sands with light,
Far off by furthest Rosses
We foot it all the night,
Weaving olden dances,
Mingling hands and mingling glances
Till the moon has taken flight ;
To and fro we leap
And chase the frothy bubbles,
While the world is full of troubles
And is anxious in its sleep.
Come away, O human child !
To the waters and the wild
With a faery, hand in hand,
For the world's more full of weeping than you
can understand.

Where the wandering water gushes
From the hills above Glen-Car,
In pools among the rushes
That scarce could bathe a star,
We seek for slumbering trout,
And whispering in their ears

Give them unquiet dreams ;
Leaning softly out
From ferns that drop their tears
Over the young streams.
Come away, O human child !
To the waters and the wild
With a faery, hand in hand,
For the world's more full of weeping than you
*   can understand.*

Away with us he's going,
The solemn-eyed :
He'll hear no more the lowing
Of the calves on the warm hillside ;
Or the kettle on the hob
Sing peace into his breast,
Or see the brown mice bob
Round and round the oatmeal-chest.
For he comes, the human child,
To the waters and the wild
With a faery, hand in hand,
From a world more full of weeping than he
*   can understand.*

William Butler Yeats.

127. THE VOICE

THE wind blows out of the gates of the day,
    The wind blows over the lonely of heart,
And the lonely of heart is withered away,
While the faeries dance in a place apart,

Shaking their milk-white feet in a ring,
Tossing their milk-white arms in the air ;
For they hear the wind laugh, and murmur and sing
Of a land where even the old are fair,
And even the wise are merry of tongue ;
But I heard a reed of Coolaney say,
" When the wind has laughed and murmured and sung,
The lonely of heart is withered away ! "

William Butler Yeats.

128. THE THREE STRANGERS

FAR are those tranquil hills,
   Dyed with fair evening's rose
On urgent, secret errand bent,
   A traveller goes.

Approach him strangers three,
Barefooted, cowled ; their eyes
Scan the lone, hastening solitary
   With dumb surmise.

One instant in close speech
With them he doth confer :
God-sped, he hasteneth on,
   That anxious traveller . . .

I was that man—in a dream :
And each world's night in vain
I patient wait on sleep to unveil
   Those vivid hills again.

Would that they three could know
How yet burns on in me
Love—from one lost in Paradise—
    For their grave courtesy.
           Walter de la Mare.

129. UXBRIDGE ROAD

THE Western Road goes streaming out to seek the
    cleanly wild,
It pours the city's dim desires towards the undefiled,
It sweeps betwixt the huddled homes about its eddies
    grown
To smear the little space between the city and the
    sown :
The torments of that seething tide who is there that
    can see ?
There's one who walked with starry feet the western
    road by me !

He is the Drover of the soul ; he leads the flock of men
All wistful on that weary track, and brings them back
    again.
The dreaming few, the slaving crew, the motley caste
    of life—
The wastrel and artificer, the harlot and the wife—
They may not rest, for ever pressed by one they
    cannot see :
The one who walked with starry feet the western road
    by me.

He drives them east, he drives them west, between the
    dark and light ;
He pastures them in city pens, he leads them home at
    night.
The towery trams, the threaded trains, like shuttles
    to and fro
To weave the web of working days in ceaseless travel
    go.
How harsh the woof, how long the weft ! who shall
    the fabric see ?
The one who walked with starry feet the western road
    by me !

Throughout the living joyful year at lifeless tasks to
    strive,
And scarcely at the end to save gentility alive ;
The villa plot to sow and reap, to act the villa lie,
Beset by villa fears to live, midst villa dreams to die ;
Ah, who can know the dreary woe ? and who the
    splendour see ?
The one who walked with starry feet the western road
    by me.

Behold ! he lent me as we went the vision of the seer ;
Behold ! I saw the life of men, the life of God shine
    clear.
I saw the hidden Spirit's thrust ; I saw the race fulfil
The spiral of its steep ascent, predestined of the Will.
Yet not unled, but shepherded by one they may not
    see—
The one who walked with starry feet the western road
    by me !
                      Evelyn Underhill.

130. IMMANENCE

I come in the little things,
  Saith the Lord :
Not borne on morning wings
Of majesty, but I have set My Feet
Amidst the delicate and bladed wheat
That springs triumphant in the furrowed sod.
There do I dwell, in weakness and in power ;
Not broken or divided, saith our God !
In your strait garden plot I come to flower :
About your porch My Vine
Meek, fruitful, doth entwine ;
Waits, at the threshold, Love's appointed hour.

I come in the little things,
Saith the Lord :
Yea ! on the glancing wings
Of eager birds, the softly pattering feet
Of furred and gentle beasts, I come to meet
Your hard and wayward heart. In brown bright eyes
That peep from out the brake, I stand confest.
On every nest
Where feathery Patience is content to brood
And leaves her pleasure for the high emprize
Of motherhood—
There doth My Godhead rest.

I come in the little things,
Saith the Lord :
My starry wings

I do forsake,
Love's highway of humility to take :
Meekly I fit my stature to your need.
In beggar's part
About your gates I shall not cease to plead—
As man, to speak with man—
Till by such art
I shall achieve My Immemorial Plan,
Pass the low lintel of the human heart.

Evelyn Underhill.

131. THE BUGLER

GOD dreamed a man ;
  Then, having firmly shut
Life like a precious metal in his fist,
Withdrew, His labour done.   Thus did begin
Our various divinity and sin.
For some to ploughshares did the metal twist,
And others—dreaming empires—straightway cut
Crowns for their aching foreheads.   Others beat
Long nails and heavy hammers for the feet
Of their forgotten Lord.   (Who dare to boast
That he is guiltless ?)   Others coined it : most
Did with it—simply nothing.   (Here, again,
Who cries his innocence ?)   Yet doth remain
Metal unmarred, to each man more or less,
Whereof to fashion perfect loveliness.

For me, I do but bear within my hand
(For sake of Him our Lord, now long forsaken)
A simple bugle such as may awaken

With one high morning note a drowsing man :
That wheresoe'er within my motherland
The sound may come, 'twill echo far and wide
Like pipes of battle calling up a clan,
Trumpeting men through beauty to God's side.

F. W. Harvey.

132. THE TWILIGHT OF EARTH

THE wonder of the world is o'er :
  The magic from the sea is gone :
There is no unimagined shore,
  No islet yet to venture on.
The Sacred Hazels' blooms are shed,
The Nuts of Knowledge harvested.

Oh, what is worth this lore of age
  If time shall never bring us back
Our battle with the gods to wage
  Reeling along the starry track.
The battle rapture here goes by
In warring upon things that die.

Let be the tale of him whose love
  Was sighed between white Deirdre's breasts,
It will not lift the heart above
  The sodden clay on which it rests.
Love once had power the gods to bring
All rapt on its wild wandering.

We shiver in the falling dew,
   And seek a shelter from the storm :
When man these elder brothers knew
   He found the mother nature warm,
A hearth fire blazing through it all,
A home without a circling wall.

We dwindle down beneath the skies,
   And from ourselves we pass away ;
The paradise of memories
   Grows ever fainter day by day.
The shepherd stars have shrunk within,
The world's great night will soon begin.

Will no one, ere it is too late,
   Ere fades the last memorial gleam,
Recall for us our earlier state ?
   For nothing but so vast a dream
That it would scale the steeps of air
Could rouse us from so vast despair.

The power is ours to make or mar
   Our fate as on the earliest morn,
The Darkness and the Radiance are
   Creatures within the spirit born.
Yet, bathed in gloom too long, we might
Forget how we imagined light.

Not yet are fixed the prison bars ;
   The hidden light the spirit owns
If blown to flame would dim the stars
   And they who rule them from their thrones :

And the proud sceptred spirits thence
Would bow to pay us reverence.

Oh, while the glory sinks within
   Let us not wait on earth behind,
But follow where it flies, and win
   The glow again, and we may find
Beyond the Gateways of the Day
Dominion and ancestral sway.

A. E.

133. HOPE IN FAILURE

Though now thou hast failed and art fallen, despair
   not because of defeat,
Though lost for a while be thy heaven and weary of
   earth be thy feet,
For all will be beauty about thee hereafter through
   sorrowful years,
And lovely the dews for thy chilling and ruby thy
   heart-drip of tears.

The eyes that had gazed from afar on a beauty that
   blinded the eyes
Shall call forth its image for ever, its shadow in alien
   skies.
The heart that had striven to beat in the heart of the
   Mighty too soon
Shall still of that beating remember some errant and
   faltering tune.

For thou hast but fallen to gather the last of the secrets
    of power ;
The beauty that breathes in thy spirit shall shape of
    thy sorrow a flower,
The pale bud of pity shall open the bloom of its
    tenderest rays,
The heart of whose shining is bright with the light of
    the Ancient of Days.

A. E.

134. THE MYSTERY

HE came and took me by the hand
    Up to a red rose tree,
He kept His meaning to Himself
    But gave a rose to me.
I did not pray Him to lay bare
    The mystery to me,
Enough the rose was Heaven to smell,
    And His own face to see.

Ralph Hodgson.

135. I SEE HIS BLOOD UPON THE ROSE

I SEE His blood upon the rose
    And in the stars the glory of His eyes,
His body gleams amid eternal snows,
His tears fall from the skies.

I see His face in every flower ;
The thunder and the singing of the birds
Are but His voice—and carven by His power
Rocks are His written words.

All pathways by His feet are worn,
His strong heart stirs the ever-beating sea,
His crown of thorns is twined with every thorn,
His cross is every tree.

Joseph Mary Plunkett.

136. HE IS THE LONELY GREATNESS

HE is the lonely greatness of the world—
    (His eyes are dim),
His power it is holds up the Cross
    That holds up Him.

He takes the sorrow of the threefold hour—
    (His eyelids close),
Round Him and round, the wind—His Spirit—where
    It listeth blows.

And so the wounded greatness of the World
    In silence lies—
And death is shattered by the light from out
    Those darkened eyes.

Madeleine Caron Rock.

137. THE FINAL MYSTERY

(This myth, of Egyptian origin, formed part of the instruction
given to those initiated in the Orphic mysteries, and written versions
of it were buried with the dead.)

HEAR now, O Soul, the last command of all—
    When thou hast left thine every mortal mark,
And by the road that lies beyond recall
Won through the desert of the Burning Dark,
Thou shalt behold within a garden bright
A well, beside a cypress ivory-white.

Still is that well, and in its waters cool
White, white and windless, sleeps that cypress tree :
Who drinks but once from out her shadowy pool
Shall thirst no more to all eternity.
Forgetting all, by all forgotten clean,
His soul shall be with that which hath not been.

But thou, though thou be trembling with thy dread,
And parched with thy desire more fierce than flame,
Think on the stream wherefrom thy life was fed,
And that diviner fountain whence it came.
Turn thee and cry—behold, it is not far—
Unto the hills where living waters are.

" Lord, though I lived on earth, the child of earth,
Yet was I fathered by the starry sky :
Thou knowest I came not of the shadows' birth,
Let me not die the death that shadows die.
Give me to drink of the sweet spring that leaps
From Memory's fount, wherein no cypress sleeps."

Then shalt thou drink, O Soul, and therewith slake
The immortal longing of thy mortal thirst ;
So of thy Father's life shalt thou partake,
And be for ever that thou wert at first.
Lost in remembered loves, yet thou more thou
With them shalt reign in never-ending *Now*.

Henry Newbolt.

138. THE LAUNCH

FORTH, to the alien gravity,
    Forth, to the laws of ocean, we
  Builders on earth by laws of land
Entrust this creature of our hand
Upon the calculated sea.

Fast bound to shore we cling, we creep,
And make our ship ready to leap
    Light to the flood, equipped to ride
    The strange conditions of the tide—
New weight, new force, new world : the Deep.

Ah thus—not thus—the Dying, kissed,
Cherished, exhorted, shriven, dismissed ;
    By all the eager means we hold
    We, warm, prepare him for the cold,
To keep the incalculable tryst.

Alice Meynell.

139. EPILOGUE TO "A JUDGEMENT IN HEAVEN"

VIRTUE may unlock hell, or even
    A sin turn in the wards of Heaven,
(As ethics of the text-book go,)
So little men their own deeds know,
Or through the intricate *mêlée*
Guess whitherward draws the battle-sway ;

So little, if they know the deed,
Discern what therefrom shall succeed.
To wisest moralists 'tis but given
To work rough border-law of Heaven,
Within this narrow life of ours,
These marches 'twixt delimitless Powers.
Is it, if Heaven the future showed,
Is it the all-severest mode
To see ourselves with the eyes of God ?
God rather grant, at His assize,
He see us not with our own eyes !

Heaven, which man's generations draws,
Nor deviates into replicas,
Must of as deep diversity
In judgement as creation be.
There is no expeditious road
To pack and label men for God,
And save them by the barrel-load.
Some may perchance, with strange surprise,
Have blundered into Paradise.
In vasty dusk of life abroad,
They fondly thought to err from God,
Nor knew the circle that they trod ;
And, wandering all the night about,
Found them at morn where they set out.
Death dawned ; Heaven lay in prospect wide :—
Lo ! they were standing by His side !

                            Francis Thompson.

140. ENVOY

Go, songs, for ended is our brief, sweet play ;
   Go, children of swift joy and tardy sorrow :
And some are sung, and that was yesterday,
   And some unsung, and that may be to-morrow.

Go forth ; and if it be o'er stony way,
   Old joy can lend what newer grief must borrow :
And it was sweet, and that was yesterday,
   And sweet is sweet, though purchasèd with sorrow.

Go, songs, and come not back from your far way :
   And if men ask you why ye smile and sorrow,
Tell them ye grieve, for your hearts know To-day,
   Tell them ye smile, for your eyes know To-morrow.
                Francis Thompson.

INDEX OF FIRST LINES

171